Changes in the Standards for Admitting Expert Evidence in Federal Civil Cases Since the *Daubert* Decision

T0159716

Lloyd Dixon

Brian Gill

Prepared for the
RAND Institute for Civil Justice

RAND
INSTITUTE FOR
CIVIL JUSTICE

This research was supported by RAND Institute for Civil Justice core funds.

ISBN: 0-8330-3088-4

RAND is a nonprofit institution that helps improve policy and decisionmaking through research and analysis. RAND's publications do not necessarily reflect the opinions or policies of its research sponsors.

Published 2001 by RAND
1700 Main Street, P.O. Box 2138, Santa Monica, CA 90407-2138
1200 South Hayes Street, Arlington, VA 22202-5050
201 North Craig Street, Suite 102, Pittsburgh, PA 15213
RAND URL: http://www.rand.org/
To order RAND documents or to obtain additional information, contact Distribution Services: Telephone: (310) 451-7002; Fax: (310) 451-6915; Email: order@rand.org

THE INSTITUTE FOR CIVIL JUSTICE

The mission of the RAND Institute for Civil Justice is to improve private and public decisionmaking on civil legal issues by supplying policymakers and the public with the results of objective, empirically based, analytic research. The ICJ facilitates change in the civil justice system by analyzing trends and outcomes, identifying and evaluating policy options, and bringing together representatives of different interests to debate alternative solutions to policy problems. The Institute builds on a long tradition of RAND research characterized by an interdisciplinary, empirical approach to public policy issues and rigorous standards of quality, objectivity, and independence.

ICJ research is supported by pooled grants from corporations, trade and professional associations, and individuals; by government grants and contracts; and by private foundations. The Institute disseminates its work widely to the legal, business, and research communities, and to the general public. In accordance with RAND policy, all Institute research products are subject to peer review before publication. ICJ publications do not necessarily reflect the opinions or policies of the research sponsors or of the ICJ Board of Overseers.

RAND Institute for Civil Justice
1700 Main Street, P.O. Box 2138
Santa Monica, CA 90407-2138
(310) 393-0411 x7893

Director: Alan F. Charles
Research Director: Robert T. Reville

Westlaw is the exclusive online distributor of RAND/ICJ materials. The full text of many ICJ documents can be found at http://www.westlaw.com/. A profile of the ICJ, summaries of all its studies, and electronic order forms are on RAND's homepage on the World Wide Web at http://www.rand.org/centers/icj/.

PREFACE

In its 1993 *Daubert* decision, the U.S. Supreme Court clarified the standards judges should use in deciding whether to admit expert evidence into federal cases. The Supreme Court directed judges to evaluate the method and reasoning underlying the expert evidence and to admit only evidence that was reliable and relevant. This study examines how judges have changed the way they evaluate expert evidence since *Daubert* and how the parties proposing and challenging evidence have responded.

The research was funded by the RAND Institute for Civil Justice. It should help Congress, the Supreme Court, the Federal Rules Committee, and other policymakers better assess the current system for screening expert evidence, target areas where more detailed study is necessary, and evaluate possible reforms.

For more information about this report, contact:

Lloyd Dixon
Institute for Civil Justice
RAND
1700 Main Street
Santa Monica, CA 90407-2138
TEL: (310) 393-0411 x7480
FAX: (310) 451-6979
Email: Lloyd_Dixon@rand.org

CONTENTS

Appendix

FIGURES

TABLES

SUMMARY

The U.S. Supreme Court's 1993 *Daubert* decision clarified the standards that federal judges should use for deciding whether expert evidence is to be admitted into a case.[1] Before *Daubert*, there was not a universally followed standard for determining the admissibility of expert evidence in federal courts. The two leading standards were relevance and general acceptance in the expert community. Critics of the relevance standard argued that it let in too much "junk science" because it allowed all evidence that addressed a fact at issue in the case. Critics of the general acceptance standard argued that it excluded novel science that was quite reliable because it deferred to the current consensus in the expert community.

In *Daubert*, the Supreme Court directed federal judges to examine the method or reasoning underlying the expert evidence and to admit only evidence that was reliable and relevant. For scientific evidence, the Supreme Court considered evidence reliable if it was grounded in the methods and procedures of science. No longer can judges defer to the appropriate expert community to determine whether evidence was reliable, and no longer can they leave the determination to the jury. Judges are to act as "gatekeepers," screening expert evidence to ensure that what is admitted is both relevant and reliable.

In this report, we examine the effects of the new standards for admitting expert evidence into federal court. Our analysis provides strong evidence that the *Daubert* opinion changed how federal district court judges assess expert evidence in civil cases. It appears that judges are indeed doing what they were directed to do by the Supreme Court: they are increasingly acting as gatekeepers for reliability and relevance, they are examining the methods and reasoning underlying the evidence, and they appear to be employing general acceptance as only one of many factors that enter into their reliability assessments. The rise that took place in both the proportion of evidence found unreliable and the proportion of challenged evidence excluded suggests that the standards for admitting evidence have tightened. The subsequent fall in these two proportions suggests that parties proposing evidence—and perhaps parties challenging evidence as well—have responded to the change in standards.

ANALYTIC APPROACH

To explore the effects of *Daubert*, we statistically analyzed trends in 399 federal district court opinions issued between January 1980 and June 1999 that addressed challenges to expert evidence in civil cases. These challenges, which were brought by plaintiffs, defendants, and

---

[1]*Daubert v. Merrell Dow Pharmaceuticals, Inc.*, 509 U.S. 579 (1993).

occasionally the courts themselves, requested that the judge exclude the proposed evidence from the case. To select the opinions, we searched Westlaw's database of federal district court opinions using a search string that identified challenges to expert evidence. We then extracted detailed information from a random sample of the opinions identified. This information concerned the characteristics of the case, the nature of the evidence challenged, the characteristics of the experts, and the outcomes of the challenges. We also recorded the factors the judge discussed in assessing whether the evidence should be admitted, as well as whether the judge rated the evidence favorably, unfavorably, or neither favorably nor unfavorably on each factor.

Roughly one-third of the opinions addressed several distinct elements of expert evidence, and many addressed testimony by more than one expert. As a result, our analysis involves 601 separate elements of evidence (38 percent pre-*Daubert* and 62 percent post-*Daubert*) and 569 experts (some of whom may have appeared in more than one of the opinions examined). Many different types of cases are represented in the sample, as are many different types of evidence.[2]

The proportion of challenged evidence that is found unreliable, the proportion of evidence excluded, and other outcomes of interest are probably influenced by factors other than just the *Daubert* decision. Thus, we cannot be sure whether changes in these outcomes were due to *Daubert* or to other factors. At a minimum, our analysis documents changes over time in the outcomes of interest, but we seek evidence of *Daubert*'s effects by looking for patterns characteristic of the particulars of the *Daubert* decision.

Our analysis proceeded in two stages. In the first, we examined changes in the outcomes of interest while holding constant the case type, substantive area of evidence, and federal appellate circuit in which the district court issuing the opinion lies. In the second, we looked for signs of change in case type and substantive area of evidence.

FINDINGS

After *Daubert*, Judges Scrutinized Reliability More Carefully and Applied Stricter Standards

Federal judges apply three main criteria in deciding whether to admit evidence: reliability (whether the evidence is genuine, valid knowledge from the expert's field), relevance (whether it assists the trier of fact in determining a fact at issue), and qualifications (whether the expert has specialized knowledge relevant to the testimony). Judges may also take other factors into

---

[2]*Case type* refers to the nature of the underlying dispute, such as a product liability dispute or a dispute over employment practices. *Type of evidence* refers to the substantive area in which the evidence is based, such as toxicology or economics.

account, such as whether the evidence is unfairly prejudicial or is based on privileged information.

Our analysis of district court opinions suggests that after *Daubert*, judges scrutinized reliability more carefully and applied stricter standards in deciding whether to admit expert evidence. When case type, substantive area of evidence, and appellate circuit were held constant, we found that the proportion of rulings on challenges in which the judge discussed reliability began to rise after *Daubert* and rose steadily through mid-1997 (Figure S.1).[3] It is likely that this increase reflects an increase in the frequency with which parties challenging expert evidence targeted reliability. In cases where reliability was discussed, the proportion of evidence that was found unreliable increased through mid-1997. That is, the success rate of challenges based on reliability initially increased, suggesting that judges were applying stricter standards in assessing reliability. Taken together, these trends imply that the proportion of challenged evidence found unreliable initially rose after *Daubert*.

Judges Also Appear to Have Scrutinized Relevance, Qualifications, and Other Considerations That Enter into the Admission Decision More Carefully

The *Daubert* decision did not change the standards for judging the relevance of expert evidence, the qualifications of experts, or other considerations that enter into the assessment of expert evidence, but it did affirm that judges should act as gatekeepers. Our findings suggest that judges scrutinized these criteria, in addition to reliability, with increasing care after *Daubert*. We found that the success rates of challenges to relevance, qualifications, and other considerations (i.e., the percentage of evidence rated unfavorably on a criterion given that the criterion was addressed) rose following *Daubert* (see Figure S.2), although the increases did not always achieve statistical significance.[4] It appears that once judges began acting as more watchful gatekeepers, they more carefully examined not just reliability, but all dimensions of expert evidence.

---

[3]The reader should note that the proportions in Figure S.1 are not the observed frequencies with which reliability was addressed and evidence was found unreliable in our sample. Rather, they are the predicted probabilities for evidence based on physical science in a product liability case from a district in the Third Circuit. The average levels of trend lines would change for other combinations of case type, substantive area of evidence, and appellate circuit, but the trends over time would be similar. Likewise, the trends in Figures S.2 and S.3 are predicted probabilities, not observed frequencies.

[4]In Figure S.2, what are important are the trends over time, not the relative positions of the criteria's trends. The relative positions might change if a different case type, substantive area of evidence, and appellate circuit were used to illustrate the results.

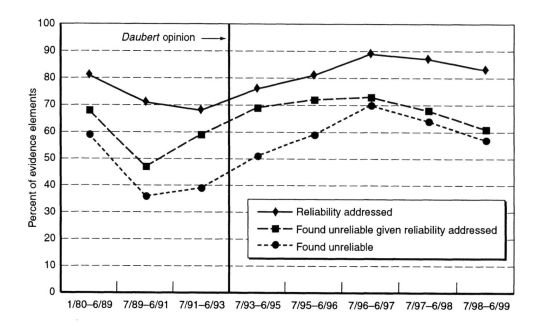

Figure S.1—Trends in Challenges to Reliability of Expert Evidence (Case Type, Substantive Area of Evidence, and Appellate Circuit Held Constant)

Challenges to Expert Evidence Became Increasingly Fatal to Cases

The closer scrutiny given to expert evidence caused an increase in the proportion of challenged evidence excluded after *Daubert*. We found, for example, that the exclusion rate in the Third Circuit for evidence based on physical science in a product liability case jumped from 53 percent during the two years before *Daubert* to 70 percent between mid-1995 and mid-1996.

Challenges also increasingly resulted in summary judgment. When we held case type, substantive area of evidence, and appellate circuit constant, we found that summary judgments were granted in 21 percent of challenges during the four years preceding *Daubert*, compared to 48 percent between July 1995 and June 1997. Over 90 percent of the summary judgments went against plaintiffs, so it is likely that challenges to plaintiffs' expert evidence increasingly resulted in dismissal of the case. The increase in summary judgments may reflect broader trends in litigation practices that have little to do with *Daubert*. But *Daubert* may have led challengers to expand their challenges to the point where they increasingly challenged the entire basis of the case. *Daubert* also may have induced a shift from dismissals based on insufficient evidence to dismissals based on inadmissible evidence.

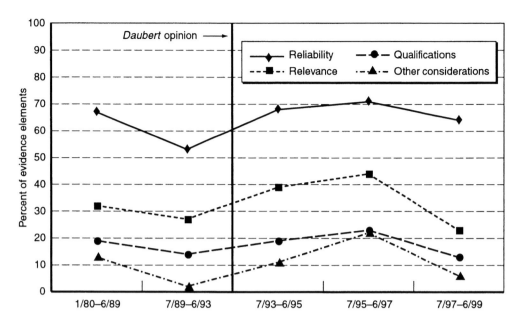

**Figure S.2—Trends in Success Rates of Challenges for Various Criteria
(Case Type, Substantive Area of Evidence, and Appellate Circuit
Held Constant)**

The Parties Responded to the Change in Standards

The parties proposing evidence and challenging evidence appear to have responded gradually to the change in standards. The percentage of challenged evidence found unreliable (see Figure S.1) and the percentage of challenged evidence excluded both declined after an initial rise. This pattern suggests that parties proposing evidence either did not propose or withdrew evidence not meeting the new standards, or better tailored the evidence they did propose to fit the new standards. It may also be that the higher success rates of challengers emboldened them to challenge more evidence. Casting a wider net would pull in challenges that are less likely to succeed, thus reducing the proportion of challenged evidence found unreliable.

Judges Increasingly Focused on Theory, Methods, and Procedures Underlying Expert Evidence

Initially, the judicial opinions focused on the five so-called *Daubert* factors in assessing the reliability of expert evidence.[5] We found that the frequency with which these factors were addressed began rising right after *Daubert*, continued to rise through June 1997, and then fell off

---

[5]The *Daubert* factors are what the Supreme Court discussed in the *Daubert* opinion as examples of types of factors that should enter a reliability assessment: (1) whether the theory or method can be or has been tested, (2) whether it has been subjected to peer review and publication, (3) whether it is generally accepted in the scientific community, (4) the known or potential error rate of the method, and (5) the existence and maintenance of standards controlling the method's operation.

between July 1997 and June 1999. After that, judges and challengers appear to have shifted their attention over time to factors not explicitly mentioned in the *Daubert* decision. For example, the frequency with which the clarity and coherence of the expert's explanation of the theory, methods, and procedures underlying his or her evidence were addressed did not show much increase through June 1995 but then rose rapidly through the end of the study period (July 1999).

These findings suggest that judges were at first uncertain about the proper scope of their assessment and how to go about assessing reliability. In assessing reliability, they initially focused on the five factors mentioned in the *Daubert* decision. However, as they gained experience in evaluating reliability and as appellate court opinions clarified their authority, they appear to have felt less compelled to address each *Daubert* factor and to have paid increasing attention to more-general issues important to addressing reliability.

General Acceptance Was No Longer Sufficient by Itself for Admission of Expert Evidence, But Lack of General Acceptance Remained an Important Barrier to Admission

Our findings suggest that before *Daubert*, general acceptance was not a commonly used standard for deciding whether to admit expert evidence. When it was used, however, general acceptance was a sufficient condition for admission of evidence (assuming the evidence did not fail on other criteria, such as relevance). After *Daubert*, general acceptance was not sufficient for establishing reliability. Judges sometimes found evidence unreliable even when they determined that it was generally accepted.

Our findings also suggest that lack of general acceptance was as much a barrier to admission after *Daubert* as before, and perhaps an even greater barrier. Thus, there is no indication that it became easier for novel evidence that was not generally accepted in the relevant expert community to be admitted after *Daubert*.

Judges Increasingly Examined All Types of Expert Evidence, Not Just "Hard" Science

The *Daubert* decision was issued in the context of evidence based on toxicology studies, and the Supreme Court did not explicitly discuss whether the decision applied to expert evidence more generally. In the early years after *Daubert*, there was thus uncertainty over the breadth of its applicability. We found that while judges appear to have initially focused on the "hard," or physical, sciences, they soon began to examine more closely the reliability of expert evidence in other substantive areas as well. As shown in Figure S.3, the proportion of challenged evidence

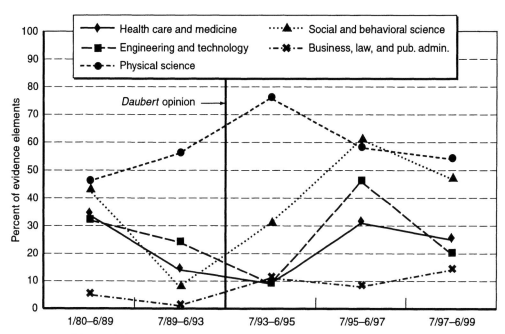

**Figure S.3—Trends in Proportion of Evidence Found Unreliable
in Various Substantive Areas of Evidence (Case Type and
Appellate Circuit Held Constant)**

found unreliable peaked just after *Daubert* for evidence based on the physical sciences. Soon thereafter, however, the proportions found unreliable for other substantive areas began to rise. It appears that once judges started evaluating reliability, they gradually began looking at all types of expert evidence.

In its 1999 *Kumho* decision,[6] the Supreme Court affirmed that judges are to act as gatekeepers for all expert evidence—not just expert evidence in the hard sciences, such as chemistry and toxicology. *Kumho* appears to have endorsed practices that were already in place in many federal courts.

Expert Evidence Based on Engineering and Technology and on Health Care and Medicine Has Increasingly Become the Target of Challenges

We have so far discussed changes we found in the standards for admitting expert evidence when case type, substantive area of evidence, and appellate circuit are held constant. However, it could be that case type and substantive area of challenged evidence themselves have changed since *Daubert*.

Our analysis did not uncover noteworthy changes in case type, but we did find systematic changes in substantive area. In the first several years after *Daubert*, the proportion of challenged evidence from the physical sciences rose. In subsequent years, it then fell and was replaced by

---

[6]*Kumho Tire Co. v. Carmichael*, 526 U.S. 137 (1999).

higher proportions of challenged evidence from engineering and technology and from health care and medicine. The initial rise in challenges to evidence from the physical sciences and the later rise in challenges to evidence from the other two areas parallel the changes that occurred over time in the percentages of each type of evidence found unreliable after *Daubert*. These patterns suggest that parties challenging evidence post-*Daubert* initially focused on the physical sciences and then moved to other areas. Challengers may have moved to other areas because the evidence based on physical science was subject to increased scrutiny and because *Daubert*'s applicability to all expert evidence became better established over time.

NEXT STEPS

Even though our findings provide strong evidence that judges have been evaluating the reliability of expert evidence more carefully since the *Daubert* decision, we are not able to determine whether outcomes have improved as a result. If judges are not accurately assessing reliability, unreliable evidence may still be admitted and reliable evidence excluded. We also have only limited information on how widespread the changes in judges' assessments of expert evidence have been across the federal bench. We conclude our analysis by identifying gaps in our understanding of how federal courts screen expert evidence and by recommending research to help fill those gaps.

How Well Are Judges Performing the Gatekeeper Function?

While judges may be more actively evaluating reliability, we do not know if they are doing it in ways that produce better outcomes. Judges may feel compelled to evaluate reliability and yet not be knowledgeable enough in the relevant field to make accurate determinations. Evidence could thus be excluded because it is difficult to understand rather than because it is unreliable. And evidence could be admitted because the judge does not understand a flaw in an argument rather than because the evidence is reliable.

It is difficult to measure the performance of court policies for evaluating and admitting evidence, but given the importance of expert evidence to case outcomes and the stakes involved, it is worth the effort. One promising approach is to assemble panels of experts to evaluate expert evidence in a sample of cases. The experts would evaluate the reliability of both admitted evidence and excluded evidence so as to understand how well the screening process is working and how much variability there is across the federal bench. The results of such an evaluation could serve as the basis of a report card on how well judges are performing the gatekeeper function.

How Has *Daubert* Affected Case Outcomes?

We have limited information on what effect *Daubert* has had on case outcomes. We found that the proportion of challenges resulting in summary judgment rose after *Daubert*, but we cannot be certain what role *Daubert* played in the increase or whether cases dismissed because evidence was excluded would have been dismissed on other grounds had there not been a change in the standards for reliability. To better understand how *Daubert* has changed the standards for admitting expert evidence and the consequences of the changes, what is needed is a more complete understanding of how exclusions of expert evidence affect case outcomes. For example, one might examine how likely it is for cases to settle or be dropped once evidence is excluded, or whether plaintiffs' attorneys are able to retool an expert and succeed in admitting similar evidence in subsequent cases.

Assembling the histories of a representative sample of cases involving expert evidence would provide a rich set of data on these and related questions. The lawyers on both sides of a case could be surveyed to characterize what evidence was introduced, what was challenged, and what was admitted and excluded. The subsequent response of the parties to the exclusion or admission of evidence could then be recorded.

What Are the Time and Dollar Costs of the Current System for Screening Expert Evidence?

This study touched only briefly on the time needed to bring and resolve challenges to expert evidence and was silent on the dollar costs both to litigants and the courts. Time and dollar costs are, of course, central concerns of a judicial system that aims to be speedy and efficient, and they are also important to justice. A system that takes a very long time to resolve disputes may discourage valid claims and prevent parties from receiving the compensation they are due. And a system in which it is very expensive to prepare expert evidence and to survive *Daubert* challenges may discourage injured parties from bringing small but valid claims.

Data on the time needed to bring and resolve challenges and the dollar costs incurred are best collected from the lawyers involved in the cases. This information could be gathered as part of the lawyer survey described above. Judicial time records could also be examined to quantify the judicial resources involved.

Answers to questions such as these are central to understanding how well the current system is working. They will help policymakers better understand the consequences of the changed standards for expert evidence, and they will help determine whether further improvements should be considered.

ACKNOWLEDGMENTS

Many people made important contributions to this project. We would particularly like to thank Judyth Pendell. During her stay at the ICJ as a visiting fellow in 1998, she identified not only the issues surrounding expert evidence in the courts but also promising research topics. Throughout the project, she provided valuable input on methodological and substantive issues and initiated contacts with others knowledgeable on expert evidence.

We benefited greatly from an advisory committee set up for the project, the members of which were

- Marsha Rabiteau (chair), Dow Chemical
- Tom Hill, General Electric
- Judyth Pendell, Pendell Consulting
- Paul Rheingold, Rheingold, Valet, Rheingold and Shkolnik, P.C.
- Paul Rothstein, Georgetown Law School
- John Shewmaker, Pfizer
- Bill Stack, Exxon Mobil.

This committee helped us interpret the trends we were seeing in the data, suggested areas for additional analysis, and provided comments on interim drafts. We thank them for their time and effort.

The formal technical reviewers of the draft report were Margaret Berger at Brooklyn Law School and Michelle White at RAND. Their comments improved the report significantly. We received insightful comments on the draft from Kim Brunner at State Farm Insurance Companies; Joe Cecil at the Federal Judicial Center; Lovida Coleman, Jr., at Sutherland, Asbill & Brennan, LLP; Tom Rowe at Duke Law School; and Larry Stewart at Stewart Tilghman Fox & Bianchi, P.A. Bert Black at Diamond McCarthy Taylor & Finley, LLP, provided insightful comments on interim findings and was a valuable source of information on expert evidence procedures, issues, and data throughout the project.

Many people at RAND made important contributions to the project. Dan McCaffrey provided statistical advice, Nick Pace helped us develop the coding instrument and access the Federal Filing Database, Steve Garber was a useful sounding board for ideas, Lisa Wong provided programming support, and Nikki Wickham formatted the coding instrument and coordinated the work of the coders. Melody Fowler, Paul Hellyer, Babak Nehoray, Eda Suh, Shaw Yadegar, and John Yang coded the opinions. We thank them for the care with which they did their work. Laura Zakaras helped improve the clarity and effectiveness of the Summary;

Robert Reville, ICJ Research Director, coordinated the review process; Pat Williams corrected and formatted interim drafts; Jeri O'Donnell did a superb job editing the document; and Joanna Nelsen did a terrific job formatting the document for publication.

Finally, we would like to thank Deborah Hensler for encouraging this line of work at the ICJ, and Alan Charles for organizing the project advisory committee and for his unflagging support throughout the project.

1. EXPERT EVIDENCE AND THE CHALLENGE FOR THE COURTS

The quality of expert evidence in the courtroom is a highly controversial subject. Expert evidence is a critical component of many types of civil litigation, and some critics have argued that too much "junk science" is admitted into evidence. In their view, juries have often been overly influenced by expert evidence that is not based on a solid scientific footing. Other critics have argued that novel expert evidence or evidence about which reasonable experts could disagree is too often barred from cases and that injured plaintiffs are not compensated as a result. In June 1993, the U.S. Supreme Court responded to the growing controversy about expert evidence by issuing the *Daubert* decision,[1] which clarified the role of federal judges as "gatekeepers" and established a new standard for how judges were to decide whether expert evidence was to be admitted. This report sheds light on how the standards for admitting expert evidence have changed since *Daubert* and how the parties proposing and challenging evidence have responded to those changes.

1.1 EVOLUTION OF STANDARDS FOR ADMISSION OF EXPERT EVIDENCE

Before *Daubert*, there was not a universally followed standard for determining the admissibility of expert evidence in the federal courts. The two leading approaches were based on relevance and general acceptance in the scientific community (Giannelli, 1994). Advocates of the relevance standard argued that expert evidence should be admitted if relevant, as long as the expert was properly qualified and admission would not prejudice or mislead the jury.[2] They believed that "junk science" could be excluded by ensuring that experts were qualified (Giannelli, 1994).[3] The general acceptance standard, also known as the *Frye* standard in reference to the 1923 federal decision that established the principle, required not only relevance and proper expert qualifications but also "general acceptance in the particular field in which it [the evidence] belongs."[4] Although the two standards were in conflict, there was little debate about the issue in the 1950s and 1960s because "controversy concerning the validity of scientific techniques did not exist at that time" (Giannelli, 1994, p. 2009).

---

[1]*Daubert v. Merrell Dow Pharmaceuticals, Inc.*, 509 U.S. 579 (1993).

[2]"'Relevant evidence' means evidence having any tendency to make the existence of any fact that is of consequence to the determination of the action more probable or less probable than it would be without the evidence" (Federal Rules of Evidence, 1997, Rule 401).

[3]Prominent texts advocating the relevance standard include McCormick (1954) and Strong (1970).

[4]*Frye v. United States*, 293 F. 1013, at 1014 (D.C. Cir. 1923).

Indeed, when the Federal Rules of Evidence were adopted in the 1970s, they did not directly address the conflict.[5] Rule 702 informs judges that expert evidence should be admitted "[i]f scientific, technical, or other specialized knowledge will assist the trier of fact to understand the evidence or to determine a fact in issue" (Federal Rules of Evidence, 1997). This could be read as consistent with either of the competing standards. In consequence, before *Daubert*, the relevance standard or the general acceptance standard continued to be the guide for admissibility decisions for expert evidence in federal court (Giannelli, 1994).

By the early 1990s, many observers felt that the existing system of judicial scrutiny of expert evidence was inadequate.[6] Scientific and technical evidence was playing a more important role in many cases,[7] and the conflict between the relevance and general acceptance standards was increasingly obvious as different federal courts came to different conclusions about the appropriate standard for admissibility (Giannelli, 1994). The relevance standard was attacked for letting in too much junk science and leaving assessment of scientific reliability entirely up to the jury.[8] Meanwhile, others argued that the general acceptance standard, by deferring to the current consensus of the expert community, excluded novel science that was quite reliable. By 1992, two experts concluded that the dispute about standards for admitting scientific evidence was the "most controversial and important unresolved question" in federal evidence law (Becker and Orenstein, 1992, p. 863).

In *Daubert v. Merrell Dow Pharmaceuticals*, the Supreme Court explained that the Federal Rules of Evidence had superseded *Frye* and that general acceptance would not be the sole standard for admissibility of expert testimony.[9] At the same time, the Court also rejected the view that all relevant testimony offered by qualified experts should be admitted. Interpreting Federal Rule of Evidence 702, the *Daubert* decision directed judges to examine the method or reasoning underlying the expert evidence and to admit only evidence that is both relevant and reliable. No longer can judges defer to the appropriate expert community to determine whether the evidence is reliable, and no longer can judges leave this determination to the jury. The

[5]*Frye* was not even discussed in the Advisory Committee's notes on Rule 702, which discusses expert testimony (Giannelli, 1994).

[6]See, for example, Huber, 1993.

[7]Data suggesting a rise in the proportion of cases involving expert evidence can be found in Section 3 of this report.

[8]This argument was made even by judges. See, e.g., *In re Joint Eastern and Southern Dist. Asbestos Litigation*, 827 F. Supp. 1014, at 1030–31 (S.D.N.Y. 1993).

[9]Jason Daubert was born with serious birth defects that he alleged were caused by his mother's ingestion of Bendectin during pregnancy. The defendants challenged plaintiffs' expert evidence that Bendectin could cause birth defects. Plaintiffs' evidence was based on animal studies, pharmacologic studies of the chemical structure of Bendectin, and the reanalysis of previously published epidemiological studies (*Daubert*, 509 U.S. 579, at 583).

Supreme Court affirmed that trial court judges have not only the "power but the *obligation* to act as a 'gatekeeper'" (Berger, 2000, p. 11), screening scientific evidence to ensure that what is admitted is both relevant and reliable.

Reliability as used by the Supreme Court refers to "evidentiary reliability—that is, trustworthiness."[10] For a case involving scientific evidence, evidentiary reliability is based on "scientific validity," which implies a grounding in the methods and procedures of science.[11] In *Daubert*, the Supreme Court provided a list of factors that judges might consider when determining whether a theory or methodology is scientifically valid:

- whether it can be (and has been) tested
- whether it has been subjected to peer review and publication
- the known or potential rate of error
- the existence and maintenance of standards controlling the technique's operation
- whether it is generally accepted in the scientific community.[12]

The Supreme Court emphasized that judges are not obligated to consider these factors (which have come to be called the *Daubert* factors) in every case and that other factors can enter their evaluations. General acceptance in the scientific community thus became only one of many factors that might enter into the assessment.

The Supreme Court confirmed and extended the *Daubert* decision in two subsequent cases. In *General Electric Co. v. Joiner* in 1997,[13] the Court examined the proper standard that appellate courts should use when reviewing a trial court's decision to admit or exclude evidence, concluding that appellate courts should not overturn the admissibility decision of a trial court unless the trial court has abused its discretion (Berger, 2000, p. 13). The Court also applied the *Daubert* approach for evaluating the reliability of scientific evidence, thus reinforcing *Daubert*. Two years later, in *Kumho Tire Co. v. Carmichael*,[14] the Court explicitly extended the *Daubert* approach to expert evidence outside fields narrowly defined as scientific. *Kumho* clarified that judges are to ensure the relevance and reliability of all expert evidence—not just expert evidence in so-called "hard" sciences, such as chemistry and toxicology. The Court also confirmed that the *Daubert* factors are illustrative of factors that judges should consider in evaluating reliability but are neither mandatory nor exhaustive (Berger, 2000, p. 16).

---

[10]*Daubert*, 509 U.S. 579, at 590 n9.
[11]*Daubert*, 509 U.S. 579, at 590.
[12]Note that the Supreme Court focused on the theory and method underlying the conclusions, not the conclusions themselves.
[13]*General Electric Co. v. Joiner*, 522 U.S. 136 (1997).
[14]*Kumho Tire Co. v. Carmichael*, 526 U.S. 137 (1999).

In December 2000, an amendment to Federal Rule of Evidence 702 took effect, its aim being to codify and clarify the principles established by the Supreme Court in *Daubert*. Rule 702 now explicitly states that in order for expert testimony to be admissible, it must be "based on sufficient facts or data," it must be "the product of reliable principles and methods," and it must involve reliable application of the principles and methods to the facts of the case (Federal Rules of Evidence, 2000).

1.2   UNCERTAINTIES ABOUT TRANSLATING DOCTRINE INTO PRACTICE

The *Daubert* decision was a major shift in legal doctrine, holding the potential for very significant consequences for plaintiffs, defendants, and the courts. The connection between official legal doctrine and the actual practice of trial courts, however, is often ambiguous.

A priori, *Daubert*'s effects are uncertain. First, there is uncertainty about how rapidly and to what degree judges would actually change their practices in response to the *Daubert* opinion. Previous research on the Civil Justice Reform Act showed that many federal courts interpreted some or all of their current or past practices as consistent with the language of the act and continued those practices unchanged (Kakalik et al., 1996, p. 10). Groscup et al. (2000, p. 4) cite articles arguing that judges would continue to use the familiar general acceptance standard while using *Daubert* terminology. In a 1998 survey of state trial court judges, Gatowski et al. (2001, p. 444) found that 38 percent of judges in states that had adopted *Daubert* believed that it had not changed their role in admitting expert evidence. Another 10 percent were unsure whether it had changed their role. (The latter two studies are described in more detail below.)

Second, there is uncertainty about whether *Daubert* raised or lowered the threshold for admitting expert evidence. By no longer requiring general acceptance, would *Daubert* lead to relaxed standards for admitting expert evidence? Or by requiring judges to examine the methods and reasoning underlying the evidence for reliability and relevance, would *Daubert* lead to tightened standards? In the eight years since *Daubert*, most observers have concluded that standards have been tightened, but the evidence for this has been only anecdotal.

Third, there is uncertainty about whether judges, in spite of their best intentions, have the time or training to carry out their gatekeeper responsibilities effectively. In their dissent to part of the *Daubert* opinion, Chief Justice Rehnquist and Justice Stevens were concerned that the opinion requires federal judges to become "amateur scientists" and to make important rulings on evidence that uses terms and concepts unfamiliar to at least some of them.[15] These concerns were substantiated, at least at the state trial court level, by the Gatowski et al. (2001, p. 442) finding

---

[15]*Daubert*, 590 U.S. 579, at 601.

that 48 percent of state court judges felt they had not been adequately prepared to handle the range of scientific evidence proffered in their courtrooms. As a result, reliable evidence may be improperly excluded, and unreliable evidence may be improperly admitted.[16]

Given these multiple uncertainties, it is important to try to understand how trial courts actually assess the admissibility of expert evidence and what *Daubert*'s effects have been in practice. Congress, the Supreme Court, the Federal Rules Committee, and other policymakers need to understand how well the post-*Daubert* system for screening expert evidence is working and what further improvements might be warranted. Policymakers need to understand the consequences of past changes so that if and when they want to make new changes, they will be informed about what types of changes work and what types do not.

1.3   PREVIOUS RESEARCH

Although *Daubert* has spawned an explosion of law review articles, treatises, newspaper reports, and even training materials for judges, very little systematic evidence on its empirical effects has been produced. Most of the academic literature has been conventional legal scholarship, involving interpretation of and commentary on *Daubert* and subsequent appellate opinions on expert evidence. Little information is available on the implementation of *Daubert* at the trial level, or more generally on how judges in lower courts assess the admissibility of expert evidence.

We are aware of only three studies that have sought systematic empirical information on the use of expert evidence in the wake of *Daubert*. First, the Federal Judicial Center (FJC) surveyed 303 federal district court judges in 1998 about their most recent civil trial experience involving expert evidence (Johnson, Krafka, and Cecil, 2000). This 1998 survey followed a similar one that took place in 1991, before the *Daubert* decision. The FJC found that judges were less likely to admit expert evidence in 1998 than in 1991: 59 percent of judges had allowed without limitation all expert evidence proffered in their last civil trial in 1998, whereas 75 percent had done so in 1991. The FJC also surveyed the lawyers involved with the trials in the 1998 survey about how their practices had changed since *Daubert*. The most common response (chosen by 32 percent of the respondents): "I made more motions *in limine* to exclude opposing experts" (p. 4).

---

[16]Another potentially important uncertainty concerns *Daubert*'s impact on the cost of proposing and challenging expert evidence and the resulting consequences for the ability of parties to submit, and for that matter to challenge, expert evidence. High costs of qualifying expert evidence may discourage injured parties with small but valid claims. A *New York Times* article linked the recent drop in product liability cases with the increased expenditures plaintiffs must make for experts in order to win cases (Winter, 2001). The *Daubert* decision may thus have implications not foreseen or intended when it was issued.

A second study, by Gatowski et al. (2001), was also based on a 1998 survey, but this one was directed at state trial court judges across the nation. It asked their views on the *Daubert* opinion and their gatekeeper responsibilities, the utility of the *Daubert* factors as decisionmaking guidelines, their understanding of the scientific meaning of the *Daubert* factors, and their application of the *Daubert* factors in practice. Four hundred judges participated in this survey, roughly evenly divided between states that followed *Daubert* and the Federal Rules of Evidence and states that followed *Frye* or hybrid approaches. The results indicate uncertainty over *Daubert*'s effects. Judges in the states following the Federal Rules were asked if they thought that their gatekeeper role had changed as a result of *Daubert*. About 50 percent said that it had, and about 50 percent said that it had not or that they were unsure whether it had (p. 444). There was also no consensus on whether the intent of *Daubert* was to raise, lower, or leave unchanged the threshold for admissibility: 32 percent said the intent was to raise it, 23 percent said the intent was to lower it, 36 percent said the intent was neither to raise nor lower it, and 11 percent were uncertain.

Gatowski et al. also found that an overwhelming proportion of judges (91 percent) supported the gatekeeper function, but that state court judges did not have a good understanding of the scientific meaning of the *Daubert* standards or how to apply them. The authors concluded that their findings question "the ability of the courts, particularly the state trial courts, to assess the scientific reliability and validity of proferred scientific evidence and hints at the potential for inconsistencies in *Daubert*'s application, especially after the *Kumho* decision" (p. 453).

The third study, by Groscup et al. (2000), examined federal and state appellate court decisions discussing expert testimony in criminal cases between 1988 and 1998. The study's authors collected data on the number of words addressing different issues related to expert evidence and the importance of the different factors entering the admissibility assessment (as viewed by the coders) in 693 appellate opinions. Based on the increased length of discussion of various federal rules of evidence addressing expert evidence, the authors inferred that appellate courts did increase their scrutiny of expert evidence after *Daubert*. However, they found no change in the proportion of evidence admitted after *Daubert* (p. 8), although there was a marginally significant decline in the proportion of "scientific" expert evidence (as distinguished from technical, health, and business-related expert evidence) admitted. They found that the attention paid to *Frye* and general acceptance fell after *Daubert*, but they did not find increases in the attention paid to the other *Daubert* factors or in the discussion of research methods. Finally, Groscup et al. found that satisfaction of the *Daubert* factors was not a good predictor of whether evidence is admitted, and they concluded that contrary to the Supreme Court's suggestion, these factors were not being used to evaluate expert testimony.

1.4   CONTRIBUTION OF THIS STUDY

This study's goal is to examine how standards for admitting expert evidence have evolved since *Daubert*. We seek signs that the standards have changed using a lens different from what was used in previous empirical studies—i.e., we look at federal district court opinions on challenges to expert evidence in civil cases. We systematically examine a relatively large number of opinions (399) issued between 1980 and 1999 in cases involving expert evidence, regardless of whether the case has gone to trial and, if it has gone to trial, regardless of whether the trial court decision has been appealed.[17]

Our approach has some advantages and some disadvantages, making it complementary to previous approaches. On the one hand, the cases we examine are in some ways more representative of the overall experience with expert evidence than are the cases used in previous studies, because few cases go to trial and few are appealed. On the other, we only examine evidence that has been challenged, whereas the Johnson, Krafka, and Cecil study (2000) looked at evidence in the last civil trial, whether challenged or not. We use information from this different source to better understand changes in standards over time and to resolve some of the conflicts among existing studies.

Our analysis of written opinions allows us to identify changes in

- types of expert evidence challenged
- criteria used to evaluate expert evidence
- reasons expert evidence is excluded
- proportion of challenged evidence excluded
- types of challenged evidence excluded.

We use the observed changes to make inferences about *Daubert*'s effects. In particular, we use these data to gain insight into

- whether judges have more carefully scrutinized the reliability and relevance of expert evidence since *Daubert*
- how the factors used in assessing reliability have changed over time
- how broadly judges applied *Daubert* in the years prior to *Kumho*—i.e., whether they applied it to "hard" science narrowly defined or to expert evidence more generally
- how the parties proposing and challenging evidence responded to changes in the criteria for screening expert evidence

---

[17]In contrast, the Johnson, Krafka, and Cecil study (2000) examined evidence in the last civil trial, and the Groscup et al. study (2000) evaluated appellate decisions.

- how the types of evidence challenged and the types of cases in which evidence is challenged have changed since *Daubert*.

Our approach allows us to evaluate how the standards that federal district judges use to evaluate expert evidence have changed, but it does not allow us to determine whether the change has produced better outcomes. Judges, for example, may feel compelled to make decisions on whether evidence is reliable but may not have the time or knowledge to make accurate determinations. The result may be no improvement, and potentially even deterioration, in system performance. Our approach does not allow us to observe the frequency with which unreliable evidence is excluded or reliable evidence admitted. Measurement of such outcomes over time would perhaps be the best way to evaluate the performance of the current system and to determine whether changes in the criteria and procedures for screening expert evidence are necessary. However, our analysis does shed light on whether judges are implementing the Supreme Court's directive to evaluate relevance and reliability, as well as what some of the consequences of a more active gatekeeper role have been. It also provides guidance for analyses in the future that are more far-reaching.

1.5   REPORT ORGANIZATION

Section 2 presents a conceptual analysis of *Daubert*'s impacts. It examines how the outcomes of challenges to expert evidence might be expected to change over time, setting the stage for our empirical analysis. Section 3 details the data used in our analysis and our analytical methods. Sections 4 through 7 present our empirical findings: Section 4 examines trends in the frequency with which judges evaluate reliability and find evidence unreliable; Section 5 drops down one level of detail to examine trends in the factors that enter the reliability assessment; Section 6 examines trends in the criteria other than reliability (i.e., relevance, qualifications, and other considerations) that are used to assess expert evidence; and Section 7 focuses on the consequences of challenges, examining changes in the proportion of challenged evidence excluded, the frequency with which summary judgment is requested and granted, and the types of evidence challenged. Section 8 then summarizes the conclusions we drew from our analysis and suggests areas for further investigation. Four appendices provide additional details on the characteristics of our sample of challenged evidence and the methods used in our analysis.

2. CONCEPTUAL ANALYSIS OF *DAUBERT*'S IMPACT ON DISPOSITION OF CHALLENGED EVIDENCE AND TYPE OF EVIDENCE CHALLENGED

Our study looks for signs of *Daubert*'s impact by comparing the changes in the disposition of challenged evidence and the type of evidence challenged before and after the decision. In this section, we examine conceptually how *Daubert* might affect the disposition of challenges and the type of evidence challenged in order to provide a framework for assessing the empirical information presented in Sections 4 through 7.

We first describe the roles of the various parties involved in introducing, challenging, and evaluating expert evidence. We then explore how *Daubert* might change the proportion of both challenged evidence found unreliable and challenged evidence excluded over time under different assumptions about the behavior of the various parties involved. Finally, we explore how *Daubert* might change the type of evidence that is challenged and the types of cases in which challenges are brought.

2.1 PARTIES INVOLVED IN PROPOSING, CHALLENGING, AND ASSESSING EXPERT EVIDENCE

Plaintiffs and defendants introduce expert evidence to bolster their case. Whether and what type of expert evidence is introduced depend on expectations about the probability that the evidence will be challenged and, if challenged, the probability that it will be admitted. The decision to propose expert evidence also depends on expectations about the effect the evidence will have on the outcome of the case if it is admitted and the costs of preparing expert evidence and fending off challenges.

Parties that challenge expert evidence presumably also weigh the cost of a challenge against the expectation that the challenge will succeed and the effect that exclusion of the evidence will have on the outcome of the case. The expectation that the challenge will be successful is based on perceptions about the standards judges apply in evaluating expert evidence and experience with similar challenges in the past. Challengers must also decide the basis on which to challenge the evidence.[1]

Judges decide whether challenged expert evidence should be admitted. They may use three major criteria in making this decision:

- Reliability: Is the evidence genuine, valid knowledge from the expert's field?
- Relevance: Will the evidence assist the trier of fact in determining a fact at issue?

---

[1]The incentives facing parties proposing and challenging expert evidence are analogous to those that enter the decision to settle out of court or go to trial. For a discussion of these incentives, see Cooter and Marks, 1982.

- Qualifications: Does the expert have specialized knowledge in the field relevant to the testimony?

Judges may also take other factors into account in their decision, such as whether the evidence is unfairly prejudicial (Rule 403 in the Federal Rules of Evidence) or is based on privileged information. Practitioners we interviewed believed that judges usually restrict their evaluations of expert evidence to the issues raised by the challengers, but that they sometimes examine issues not raised by the challengers and occasionally even initiate challenges to expert evidence themselves.

The exclusion of expert evidence can lead to a number of different outcomes and responses by the parties. It can lead to summary judgment,[2] to settlement, or to the plaintiff dropping the case. It can also lead plaintiffs to take similar cases to state courts that have different standards for admitting expert evidence.

2.2 CHANGE IN PROPORTION OF CHALLENGED EVIDENCE FOUND UNRELIABLE

If *Daubert* changed the standards for the reliability of expert evidence, one might expect to see a change in the proportion of challenged evidence found unreliable. In this section, we first explore how the proportion of challenged evidence found unreliable might change if the behavior of the parties proposing and challenging expert evidence does not change. By this we mean that the parties proposing evidence do not change the quality of the evidence proposed and that the parties challenging the evidence do not change the set of evidence challenged. We then explore what might be observed if proposers and challengers respond to the change in standards for admitting evidence.

Scenario Assuming No Response by Proposers and Challengers

Figure 2.1 shows the results when post-*Daubert* reliability standards for expert evidence are assumed to grow stricter and neither the quality of the proposed evidence nor the types of evidence challenged change. For this scenario, the share of challenged evidence found unreliable would gradually increase over time. Analogously, if *Daubert*'s effect were to *relax* the standard for admitting expert evidence, the proportion of challenged evidence found unreliable would fall over time.

---

[2]Summary judgment is a judgment granted by the court on a claim about which there is no genuine issue of material fact and upon which the party requesting the summary judgment is entitled to prevail as a matter of law. A summary judgment can dispose of all or only a portion of the issues in a case, the latter situation being referred to as a partial summary judgment (*Black's Law Dictionary*, 7th edition, West Publishing, 1999).

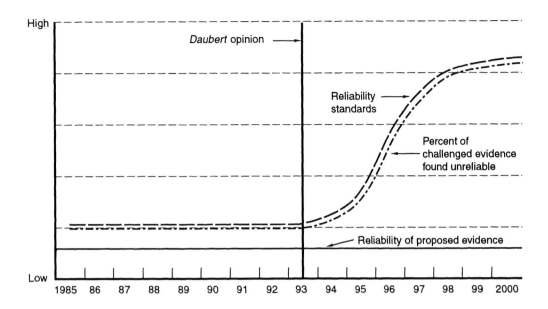

Figure 2.1—Change in Proportion of Challenged Evidence Found Unreliable When Parties Proposing and Challenging Expert Evidence Do Not Respond to Change in Reliability Standards

Scenario Assuming Response by Parties Proposing Evidence

When faced with higher rejection rates, parties that propose expert evidence may improve the quality of their evidence. For example, higher exclusion rates may induce parties to drop certain types of evidence and improve the quality of others.

Figure 2.2 illustrates a scenario in which *Daubert* tightens the standards for reliability and parties proposing expert evidence gradually respond by improving the reliability of the evidence introduced. The behavior of challengers and the set of evidence challenged do not change. In such a scenario, the proportion of evidence found unreliable first increases and then, as the quality of evidence introduced rises, declines. The extent to which the proportion of challenged evidence found unreliable rises and the speed at which it falls depend on how quickly parties proposing the evidence respond to the stricter standards. In the extreme case, proposers instantly respond to the change, and the proportion of challenged evidence found unreliable does not change at all.

A similar rise and fall in the proportion of challenged evidence found unreliable would result if proposers initially believed that *Daubert* would relax standards for admitting expert evidence and began introducing more unconventional and fringe evidence. If it turned out that standards were not relaxed, the proportion of challenged evidence excluded would then rise over time as this evidence was turned away.

-12-

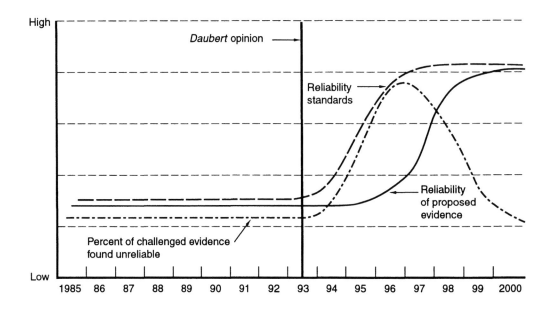

**Figure 2.2—Change in Proportion of Challenged Evidence Found Unreliable When
Parties Proposing Expert Evidence Respond to Change in Reliability Standards**

Scenarios Assuming Response by Challengers

Challengers may also respond to the change in standards for admitting evidence. If the
success rate of their challenges were to rise, they might expand the overall proportion of evidence
they challenge. An increase in the proportion of evidence challenged would likely then cause
their success rate to fall.[3] This decline would reinforce any fall in the proportion of challenged
evidence excluded due to proposers improving the quality of the evidence they introduce.

Challengers might also anticipate a tightening of standards and thus increase the
proportion of evidence challenged before the success rate of their challenges has risen. In this
scenario, the proportion of challenged evidence found unreliable might not change, even in the
face of a tightening of standards.

Summary

These scenarios indicate that a number of changes in the proportion of challenged evidence
found unreliable are possible when reliability standards tighten. The examples range from a
sustained rise to no change. The interplay of responses by proposers, challengers, and judges
makes it difficult to definitively determine *Daubert*'s impact based on data solely on challenges
to expert evidence (as opposed to data on all evidence, whether challenged or not). Our analysis

---

[3]Challengers presumably first challenge the evidence that has the highest likelihood of being
excluded, so as the proportion of evidence challenged increases, the success rate falls.

examines the data from many different angles to suggest the effects that are most plausible given what we observed.

2.3   CHANGE IN PROPORTION OF CHALLENGED EVIDENCE EXCLUDED

As will be seen in subsequent sections, expert evidence found unreliable is almost always excluded. Thus, other things being equal, changes in the proportion of challenged evidence excluded will track changes in the proportion of evidence found unreliable. However, as discussed above, criteria other than just reliability enter into a judge's decision to exclude evidence, so the change in the proportion of evidence excluded will depend on the change in how the evidence measures up against all the criteria taken together.

Because multiple criteria enter the decision to admit or exclude evidence, there may be no change in the proportion of evidence excluded even if the proportion of evidence found unreliable increases. The increase in the proportion of challenged evidence found unreliable may represent a shift in terminology or a shift in focus, rather than any real change in the standards for admitting evidence. For example, judges that might have framed concerns about a piece of evidence in terms of relevance prior to *Daubert* might now frame the same concerns in terms of reliability. If so, the proportion of challenged evidence found unreliable would rise while the proportion found irrelevant fell, but the proportion of evidence excluded would not change. In the analysis that follows, we look for evidence to distinguish whether changes after *Daubert* represented a simple shift in terminology or a real change in standards.

2.4   CHANGE IN TYPE OF EVIDENCE CHALLENGED

Changes in the standards for admitting expert evidence might induce changes in the mix of expert evidence challenged or the types of cases in which expert evidence is challenged. For example, the proportion of challenged evidence based on engineering analysis may rise if increases in the exclusion rate for engineering evidence induce challengers to more aggressively attack such evidence. Product liability cases that depend on engineering evidence may then also account for a higher fraction of cases in which evidence is challenged.

While changes in standards for admitting expert evidence may well change the mix of challenged evidence, the direction of the change is uncertain because the reactions of parties proposing and challenging evidence work in offsetting directions. For instance, in response to higher exclusion rates for engineering evidence, proposers may reduce the amount or improve the quality of the engineering evidence they propose. Other things remaining equal, this response would reduce the proportion of challenged evidence that is based on engineering. Challengers, however, might respond to the increased exclusion rate by challenging a larger proportion of the engineering evidence proposed, which would tend to increase the share of engineering evidence in challenged evidence as a whole. The result is an indeterminate change in the share of challenged evidence that is engineering-based evidence. Our analysis considers changes in the mix over time, combined with what we know about the types of evidence the *Daubert* decision might have initially targeted, to interpret any changes in the mix observed.

3. DATA AND METHODS

This section details the data used in our analysis and our analytic approach. We start by describing how we selected federal district court opinions addressing challenges to expert evidence and how we extracted the salient information from them. We then provide an overview of the opinions in our sample and conclude by describing the methods used to analyze them.

3.1   SELECTION OF OPINIONS AND DATA EXTRACTION

Westlaw Database of Federal District Court Opinions

We drew our sample of opinions from Westlaw's database of federal district court opinions. Figure 3.1 puts the Westlaw database into a broad perspective. Excluding prisoners' petitions, social security cases, and cases in which the federal government is attempting to recover debts,[1] roughly 160,000 civil cases are filed in federal court each year. The proportion of cases that involve expert evidence is unknown, as is the proportion of expert evidence that is challenged. Roughly 150 opinions addressing challenges to expert evidence in civil cases appear in Westlaw's database of federal district court opinions each year.

Westlaw provides a readily accessible source of district court opinions that can be searched in electronic form, but its limitations should be understood. First, Westlaw contains only written opinions, as opposed to oral rulings on challenges to expert evidence from the bench. The proportion of opinions on challenges to expert evidence that are written versus oral is unknown. It seems likely, however, that exclusion of expert evidence is more likely to lead to an appealable issue and that judges thus may issue written opinions more frequently when they exclude challenged evidence than when they admit it. The frequency with which evidence is excluded will likely be higher in the Westlaw database than for all opinions. This is not a problem for our analysis as long as there is no systematic change over time in the relative propensities of judges to issue written opinions when evidence is excluded versus when it is admitted. We return to this issue in Subsection 4.1.

Second, some written district court opinions are not reported to Westlaw. While Westlaw contains all officially published opinions (such as those appearing in the Federal Supplement) and a substantial number of "unreported" opinions submitted by judges, an unknown number of written opinions never appear in Westlaw. The proportion of opinions reported versus unreported

---

[1]These types of administrative cases seldom involve expert evidence.

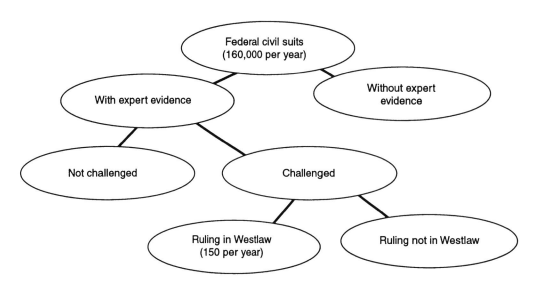

**Figure 3.1—Relation Between Opinions on Expert Evidence in Westlaw
and Federal Civil Filings**

and the coverage of unreported opinions in Westlaw likely vary by district.[2] It is also likely that the written opinions appearing in Westlaw address challenges to expert evidence that are more controversial, more precedent-setting than those addressed by written opinions not appearing in Westlaw.

Finally, opinions in Westlaw addressing expert evidence focus on disputed issues. The Westlaw database thus does not provide information on cases in which expert evidence is used but not disputed.

Even with these shortcomings, the opinions in Westlaw provide a useful source of information for analyzing changes in the standards for admitting expert evidence over time. It should be remembered, however, that our analysis examines the effects of changes on only one piece of the picture—written opinions on challenges to expert evidence that showed up in Westlaw.

Selection of Opinions

We developed an electronic search string to identify opinions in Westlaw that address challenges to expert evidence.[3] The string identified opinions containing such words as

_____

[2]For example, Westlaw lists 11 districts where, beginning with dates that vary from 1985 to 1997, opinions "are available regardless of whether the case was published by West or topical service" (Westlaw Website). It is not clear, however, whether this means that all written opinions in those districts after the dates cited are contained in Westlaw or that more than just reported opinions are included.

[3]We used this search string: (((("702" OR "703") /6 (EXPERT or EVID! or RULE)) or ((ADMISS! or INADMISS! or ADMIT! or EXCLUD! or PRECLUD! or STRIKE or STRICKEN or UNQUALIF! or

"admissibility" within eight words of "expert", or "exclude" within eight words of "expert witness". It also identified opinions that referenced Rules 702 and 703—the rules addressing expert evidence in the Federal Rules of Evidence. The search sting did not use words such as "Daubert" and "Frye" or language from the *Daubert* opinion; we wanted to ensure we would identify both pre- and post-*Daubert* opinions in an even-handed way. The string was designed to be overly inclusive so that few opinions addressing expert evidence would be missed.[4]

Our search string selected 4,097, or about 1.3 percent, of the 315,000 federal district court opinions in Westlaw that were issued between January 1980 and June 1999 (see Table 3.1).[5] Examination of a random sample of these cases revealed that roughly 30 percent were opinions in *civil* cases that addressed challenges to expert evidence.[6] We thus estimate that about 0.4 percent of the opinions (both civil and criminal) in Westlaw address challenges to evidence in civil cases.[7]

Figure 3.2 shows the estimated number and percentage of opinions in Westlaw that address challenges to expert evidence in civil cases over time. The number of opinions rose from a very low number per year in the early 1980s to nearly 150 per year at the end of the 1990s. This rise may be partly due to an increase in the total number of opinions in Westlaw's database, but Figure 3.2 also shows that the percentage of opinions addressing expert evidence rose. The increase in the percentage of opinions addressing expert evidence may be due to several factors, including (1) increasing use of expert evidence in civil litigation, (2) increasing challenges to expert evidence, (3) a rise in the proportion of opinions in Westlaw that are civil versus criminal, and (4) increasing controversy over expert evidence, leading judges to write up their opinions in this area more frequently.

Both the number and the percentage of opinions addressing challenges to expert evidence in civil cases dropped below their previous trends in 1993 and 1994 and then recovered in 1995.

DISQUALIF! or QUALIF! or BAR or BARRED or BARRING) /8 (EXPERT /3 (WITNESS or TESTI! or AFFIDAVIT)))) & DA(>12/31/1979).

[4]The search string was not limited to opinions issued pre-trial. Thus, opinions on motions to exclude evidence post-trial could also be selected.

[5]About 50,000 new district court opinions were added to the Westlaw database per year in the second half of the 1990s.

[6]We restricted our attention to substantive, as opposed to procedural, challenges to expert evidence.

[7]The percentage of opinions identified by the search string that addressed challenges to expert evidence in civil cases (true positives) increased between 1980 and 1999. To estimate the number of civil cases in Westlaw that addressed expert evidence over time, we fit a time trend to the observed true positive rates. The resulting regression was $TP = 0.192 + .00898t$, where TP is the true positive rate and t is (year − 1981). Due to the small number of observations, the data between 1980 and 1984 were aggregated and assigned to 1982.

Table 3.1

Number of Opinions Identified, Examined, and Selected

	Number of Opinions
Identified by search string	4,097 of the 315,000 opinions in Westlaw (1.3 percent)
Examined	1,345 of the 4,097 opinions (33 percent, randomly selected)
Found to address challenges to expert evidence in a civil case	399 of the 1,345 opinions (30 percent)

These declines suggest that the *Daubert* decision delayed opinions on expert evidence. Plaintiffs and defendants may have delayed motions and judges may have delayed decisions in the months prior to June 1993 in anticipation of the decision. In addition, judges may have delayed opinions and parties challenging evidence may have delayed motions in the months after *Daubert* to wait for early district court and appellate court opinions clarifying how the courts were going to interpret the decision.

Data Extraction

Law students and recent law school graduates reviewed 1,345 of the opinions identified by the search string and extracted information on the 399 that actually addressed challenges to expert evidence in civil cases. Information was extracted using a detailed coding form on the

- characteristics of the case
- nature of the evidence challenged
- criteria judges addressed in evaluating the evidence
- characteristics of the experts
- outcome of the challenge.[8]

The coders were given definitions of and examples of the concepts, terms, and information to look for in the opinions and were trained over multiple sessions. Part of the training involved extracting information from multiple test cases and then reviewing the results as a group. During the course of the survey, all coders were regularly assigned the same opinion (approximately one out of 20 opinions examined). These audit opinions were used to review the performance of coders and to correct any misunderstanding of the relevant concepts.

Since opinions often addressed distinct pieces of expert evidence, data for each element of evidence discussed were extracted separately. For example, a judge might address a challenge to the valuation of lost profits or wages in one part of the opinion and a challenge to toxicological

---

[8]The coding form is available from the authors upon request.

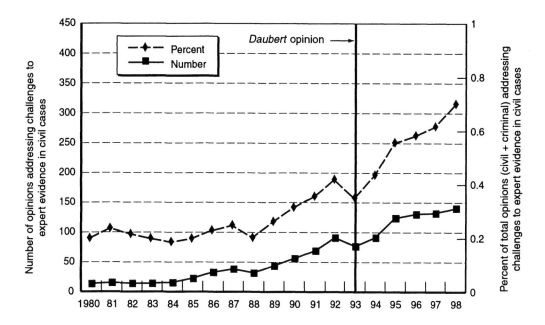

Figure 3.2—Estimated Number and Percentage of Opinions in Westlaw That Address Challenges to Expert Evidence

evidence in another. We instructed the coders to be driven by the structure of the opinion in deciding whether judges addressed multiple elements of evidence. If a judge discussed different pieces of evidence separately and made separate decisions on them, the different pieces were treated as separate elements of evidence.

The training, area of expertise, and other characteristics of each expert mentioned in the opinion were also recorded when available. The opinions were coded between July 1999 and April 2000.

3.2 OVERVIEW OF OPINIONS ANALYZED

As shown in the first row of Table 3.2, roughly one-third of the 399 opinions addressed more than one element of evidence, with the result that there are 601 separate elements of evidence in our sample (38 percent pre-*Daubert*, 62 percent post-*Daubert*). Information was collected on 569 experts (some of whom may have appeared in more than one of the opinions examined).

The 399 opinions were written by 263 different judges spread across 71 of the 94 federal court districts.[9] All federal appellate circuits were represented in the sample. Appendix A details

---

[9]There are currently 665 authorized district court judgeships, of which 76 are vacant. See http://www.uscourts.gov/vacancies/summary.html.

Table 3.2

**Number of Coded Opinions, Elements of Evidence, and Experts,
and Number of Represented Federal Court Districts and Judges**

	Pre-*Daubert* (1/80–6/93)	Post-*Daubert* (7/93–6/99)	Total
Opinions	163	236	399
Elements of evidence	226	375	601
Experts	206	363	569
Districts	48	58	71
Judges	127	176	263

the breakdown of opinions by appellate circuit and compares it with the distribution of federal civil filings.

The challenges were largely brought by defendants (76 percent), and the challenged evidence was largely proposed by plaintiffs (80 percent). Rarely did courts initiate challenges themselves.[10] Most defendants were businesses (70 percent), and most plaintiffs were individuals (73 percent). About one-half of the cases alleged physical or emotional human harm; the rest mainly alleged financial harm. Over 70 percent of the opinions were issued pre-trial, and a jury, rather than the judge, was usually expected to be the trier of fact.

Appendix A contains more detail on the characteristics of the cases, the challenged evidence, the experts, and the litigants. The following subsections describe the nature of the dispute underlying the case—i.e., the case type—and the substantive area of the challenged evidence, information we use subsequently in exploring changes in the standards for admitting expert evidence since *Daubert*.

Case Type

Table 3.3 breaks down the 601 elements of evidence in our sample by case type. Approximately 23 percent are from product liability cases alleging bodily injury or property damage. Other forms of bodily injury and property damage torts account for another 24 percent. Contract disputes and business torts also underlie a sizeable fraction of the elements of evidence.[11] In Appendix A, we compare case type for the opinions in our sample with case type

---

[10]Johnson, Krafka, and Cecil (2000, p. 4) also found that judges rarely raise a question of admissibility when it is not disputed by the parties.

[11]Johnson, Krafka, and Cecil (2000) found that 45 percent of federal civil trials involving expert evidence were tort cases (47 percent of the 601 elements of evidence we examined were from tort cases). The biggest difference in the two samples is that 23 percent of their trials were civil rights cases, whereas only 7 percent of the evidence elements here were. Their trials occurred around 1998, and part of the difference may be due to an increase in civil rights cases over time. It may also be that a higher percentage of civil rights cases go to trial.

Table 3.3

Types of Cases in Which Expert Evidence Challenged

Case Type	Number	Percent
Bodily injury and property damage (BI and PD) torts	280	47
Product Liability	137	23
Asbestos related	9	2
Motor-vehicle related	24	4
Medical drugs and devices	32	5
Other product liability	72	12
Toxic torts	50	8
Professional negligence	62	10
Medical malpractice	23	4
Other professional negligence	39	6
Other negligence or tort (not related to business practices)	31	5
Contract cases and business torts	91	15
Intellectual property	47	8
Antitrust	22	4
Employee relations/discrimination	29	5
Civil rights (not employment related)	42	7
Securities	10	2
Other and unknown	80	13
Total	601	100

for all federal civil filings. The findings suggest that challenges to expert evidence occur more frequently in product liability, medical malpractice, and intellectual property cases than in other types of cases.

Substantive Area of Evidence

The expert evidence in the opinions we analyzed covered a wide range of substantive areas. As shown in Table 3.4, the evidence is fairly evenly spread across five major areas.[12,13]

---

[12]The substantive area of evidence describes the subject area of the evidence, not the training of the expert. Health care and medicine covers evidence pertaining to the diagnosis and treatment of illness or injury. Included is all evidence based on medical specialties (such as oncology or orthopedics), dentistry, drug addiction diagnosis and treatment, nursing, pharmacy, physical therapy, x-ray use and interpretation, etc. Engineering and technology includes evidence pertaining to such fields as products engineering, architecture, computer science, ergonomics, safety, and accident reconstruction. Physical science includes biology, epidemiology, physics, toxicology, pharmacology, mathematics, etc. Social and behavioral science includes fields such as economics (including analysis of lost profit and wages), experimental psychology, and sociology. Business, law, and public administration includes accounting, law, management, police procedures, securities and banking, etc.

[13]The distribution of evidence by substantive area here differs from that reported by Johnson, Krafka, and Cecil (2000) for federal civil trials. They found that 43 percent of the evidence was in medical and mental health, which is a much higher proportion than the 18 percent here. They also show a substantially lower proportion of evidence in physical science. These differences are likely driven by (1)

Table 3.4

Substantive Areas of Evidence

Substantive Area	Number	Percent
Health care and medicine	107	18
Engineering and technology	115	19
Physical sciences	92	15
Social and behavioral science	97	16
Business, law, and public administration	143	24
Other	18	3
Not discussed	29	5
Total	601	100

The substantive areas tended to concentrate in particular case types. Figure 3.3 shows the distribution of case type for each substantive area of evidence. Expert evidence based on engineering and technology, physical science, and health care and medicine is heavily concentrated in product liability and other bodily injury and property damage torts. Expert evidence based on social and behavioral science and on business, law, and public administration is concentrated in business and other types of cases.

3.3 ANALYTIC APPROACH

We are interested in how the *Daubert* decision changed the standards for admitting expert evidence. The ideal research design would entail a controlled experiment in which we impose the *Daubert* standards for admissibility in one jurisdiction while maintaining the existing standards in another. Then, if care were taken to ensure that the two jurisdictions were similar in other respects, the effect of the change in standards could be determined by comparing the outcomes of interest in the two jurisdictions over time. Of course, controlled experiments are rare in public policy and rarer still in law, where uniformity of standards is a strong norm. In fact, *Daubert* applied to all federal district courts, so we do not have the luxury of a control group, at least at the federal district court level.[14] This makes it difficult to separate changes due to *Daubert* from changes due to other factors that were changing over time.

---

differences in evidence between cases that go to trial and all cases, and (2) differences in challenged evidence and all expert evidence, whether challenged or not. (The Johnson, Krafka, and Cecil study included expert evidence in civil trials, whether it was challenged or not. Our data cover only challenged expert evidence, but include evidence for cases that did and did not go to trial.)

[14]Some state courts have adopted the *Daubert* approach and others have not. It would thus be fruitful to compare changes in these two groups of state courts. Gatowski et al. (2001) surveyed state trial court judges in states that have adopted *Daubert* and states that have not. However, for the outcomes examined, they did not find much difference between the two groups of states (p. 455).

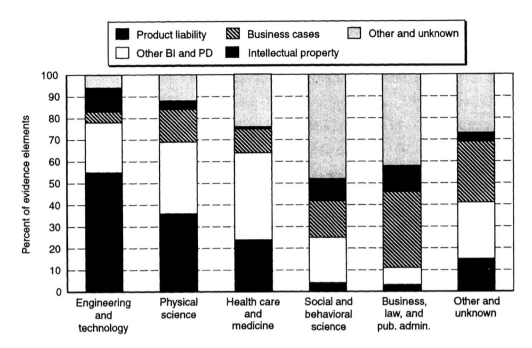

Figure 3.3—Distribution of Case Type for Expert Evidence in Different Substantive Areas

Indeed, changes in a number of factors other than *Daubert* could have affected the admissibility of expert evidence. In December 1993, just six months after the *Daubert* decision, changes affecting expert evidence were made to the Federal Rules of Civil Procedure. Rule 26(a)(2) was modified to require disclosure of expert testimony 90 days before trial in the absence of other directions from the court, and Rule 26(b)(4) was modified to require experts to furnish reports on the bases of their conclusions and to be deposed if requested. Such information provides ammunition for challenges to expert evidence. The composition of the bench has also been changing due to judge turnover. The increasing presence of perhaps more-conservative judges through appointments made by President Reagan and President Bush might have changed how courts handle evidence regardless of whether the *Daubert* decision was issued.

At a minimum, our analysis documents changes over time in the criteria used to assess evidence, the proportion of challenged evidence found unreliable, the proportion of challenged evidence excluded, and other outcomes of interest. Such information is useful for better understanding how expert evidence is handled in the courts, regardless of the reasons for the changes. We cannot be sure whether the changes were due to *Daubert* or to other factors, but we look for signs that *Daubert* was responsible.

Over the period of interest here (1980 to 1999), the case types of the opinions we examined changed, as did the substantive areas of evidence and the districts issuing the opinions. These changes could alter over time the proportion of challenged evidence excluded and other outcomes of interest even in the absence of changes in standards or procedures for evaluating expert evidence. In the first stage of our analysis, we thus use statistical techniques to estimate how the outcomes of interest—say, the proportion of challenged evidence found unreliable—changed in the years before and after *Daubert* when the non-time-varying aspects of case type, substantive area of evidence, and federal appellate circuit in which the opinion-issuing district lies are held constant. We then use the estimates to predict changes over time in the outcomes of interest for a particular case type and substantive area in a particular appellate circuit.

When presenting the results, we predict changes for evidence from the physical sciences in a product liability case. We selected this as our reference case because this combination of case type and substantive area is common in the opinions we examined and because it reflects the particular situation addressed by the *Daubert* decision itself. We predict outcomes for opinions from the Third Appellate Circuit because this is the most common circuit in our data. The level of the predictions (e.g., for the percentage of evidence found unreliable) would be different for other combinations of case type, substantive area of evidence, and appellate circuit, but the pattern over time would be similar and the statistical significance of the differences would be the same. The statistical methods used in our analysis are described in Appendix B.

As discussed in Section 2, *Daubert* may also affect the type of cases filed and the substantive areas in which evidence is grounded. Thus, in the second stage of our analysis, we examine how case type and substantive area of challenged evidence have changed over time. In sum, the first part of our analysis examines how *Daubert* has affected the outcomes of interest conditional on case type, substantive area of evidence, and appellate circuit; and the second part examines how *Daubert* has affected case type and substantive area of evidence.

4. CHANGES IN RELIABILITY STANDARDS SINCE *DAUBERT*

This section examines trends in how often federal district court judges address reliability in written opinions and how frequently evidence is found unreliable. We use the findings to draw inferences about whether judges have more actively screened evidence for reliability and about the consequences of any increased scrutiny. The evidence suggests that since *Daubert*, judges have examined the reliability of expert evidence more closely and have found more evidence unreliable as a result. Our analysis, however, does not allow us to conclude whether this increased scrutiny resulted in better outcomes.

We begin this section by examining trends over time in the frequency with which reliability is addressed in the written opinions and the proportion of challenged evidence that is found unreliable. We then explore how broadly *Daubert* has been applied in order to determine whether judges have restricted their attention to the "hard" sciences addressed by the decision or have more actively examined reliability in other substantive areas as well.

4.1   TRENDS IN FREQUENCY WITH WHICH RELIABILITY IS ADDRESSED AND EVIDENCE IS FOUND UNRELIABLE

For each of the 601 elements of evidence in our sample, we recorded whether the judge addressed reliability. We considered reliability addressed if the judge evaluated the theory, methods, procedures, and logic underlying the findings or the validity of the findings themselves.[1] Reliability pertains to the trustworthiness of the evidence, not whether it is relevant to the particular case.[2] The proportion of evidence in which reliability is addressed in large part reflects the proportion of evidence in which reliability is questioned by challengers. Parties challenging evidence likely raise the issue of reliability only when questioning it, and judges by and large address reliability only when challengers question it.

In addition, we recorded whether the judge found the evidence unreliable. The proportion of challenged evidence that is found unreliable reflects both the proportion of challenged evidence in which reliability is questioned and the standards applied by judges to evaluate reliability. In the discussion below, we report changes in the proportion found unreliable given that reliability was addressed. This conditional probability can be thought of as the success rate of challenges to reliability. It reflects the standards that judges apply in determining reliability (as

---

[1]A discussion of general acceptance was categorized as a discussion of reliability.
[2]Relevance is coded separately and will be discussed in Section 6, along with other criteria that judges use in deciding whether to admit expert evidence.

well as the quality of the challenged evidence) and allows us to better separate actions taken by challengers and actions taken by judges.[3]

Findings

Table 4.1 reports (second through fourth columns) trends in the frequency with which reliability was addressed and the proportion of challenged evidence found unreliable.[4] It also reports (last two columns) trends in success rates for challenges to reliability. As shown in panel A of the table, reliability was addressed for roughly 50 percent of the 601 elements of evidence. Judges found the evidence unreliable about 50 percent of the time that reliability was addressed, with the result that 26 percent of the 601 elements of evidence were found unreliable.

Panel B of Table 4.1 reports changes in percentages over time when case type, substantive area of evidence, and appellate circuit in which opinion-issuing district lies are held constant.[5] Note that these probabilities are predicted for a particular case type, substantive area of evidence, and appellate circuit.[6] The levels of the predictions would be different if other reference categories were chosen, but the trends over time would be similar. Thus, when interpreting these and other numbers produced by the same technique, the reader should focus on the trends over time and not the levels.

As can be seen from Table 4.1 and Figure 4.1, the frequency with which reliability was addressed fell before *Daubert* and then rose after *Daubert* until 1997, at which point it began to tail off. A similar pattern holds for the percentage of evidence found unreliable. The success rate of challenges to reliability rose through 1997 and then tailed off.[7] Also, changes in the success of challenges based on reliability preceded changes in the proportion of challenged evidence in which reliability was addressed.

Differences Between Evidence Proposed by Plaintiffs and Defendants. We found similar trends in the frequency with which reliability was addressed for evidence proposed by plaintiffs and by defendants, although our modest sample size of defendants' evidence did not

---

[3]The probability that evidence is found unreliable is the product of the success rate and the probability that reliablity is addressed: prob(evidence found unreliable) = prob(evidence found unreliable given that reliability addressed) * prob(reliability addressed).

[4]We broke the time periods in June of each year to line up the date of the *Daubert* decision (June 28, 1993), and we grouped years to produce an adequate number of observations in each time period.

[5]The statistical methods used to create these predictions are described in Appendix B.

[6]The probabilities are predicted for a product liability case, evidence from the physical sciences, and a district court in the Third Appellate Circuit.

[7]Changes in the success rate from the reference period (7/91–6/93) are not statistically significant. However, the smooth pattern suggests that the rise and subsequent fall in the success rate were not just random events.

Table 4.1

**Proportion of Challenged Evidence in Which Reliability Addressed and
Proportion Found Unreliable**
(percent)

Opinion Date	All Elements of Evidence			Elements of Evidence in Which Reliability Addressed	
	N	Reliability Addressed	Evidence Found Unreliable	N	Evidence Found Unreliable
A. Raw Data					
1/80–6/89	93	46	26	43	56
7/89–6/91	55	42	18	23	43
7/91–6/93	78	32	15	25	44
7/93–6/95	106	46	22	44	48
7/95–6/96	78	56	36	44	64
7/96–6/97	65	60	34	39	56
7/97–6/98	62	61	32	38	53
7/98–6/99	64	53	27	34	50
All periods	601	48	26	290	53
B. Predicted Probability (Case Type, Substantive Area of Evidence, and Appellate Circuit Held Constant)					
1/80–6/89	—	81*	59	—	68
7/89–6/91	—	71	36	—	47
7/91–6/93	—	68	39	—	59
7/93–6/95	—	76	51	—	69
7/95–6/96	—	81*	59	—	72
7/96–6/97	—	89**	70**	—	73
7/97–6/98	—	87**	64**	—	68
7/98–6/99	—	83**	57	—	61

NOTE: Reference period used to calculate statistical significance of changes is shaded. A single asterisk (*) indicates that the difference from the reference period is statistically significant at 10 percent; a double asterisk (**) indicates that the difference from the reference period is statistically significant at 5 percent.

allow as thorough an analysis as was possible for the full sample. As expected, the results for plaintiffs' evidence (80 percent of the 601 elements of evidence) mirrored the results for plaintiffs and defendants combined. The rise in how frequently reliability was addressed for defendants' evidence after *Daubert* was not statistically significant due to the modest sample size, but the magnitude of the increase was sizable.[8]

---

[8]We ran separate regressions for plaintiffs' and defendants' evidence. Because of the relatively small number of observations for defendants' evidence, the regressions divided the years into five time periods rather than the eight reported in Table 4.1 and collapsed the 11 appellate circuits into four geographic regions. For the same reason, four case-type categories and four substantive-area categories were used.

-28-

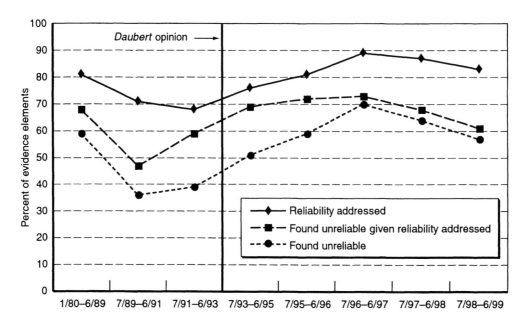

**Figure 4.1—Frequency with Which Reliability Addressed and Evidence
Found Unreliable (Case Type, Substantive Area of Evidence, and
Appellate Circuit Held Constant)**

Differences Between Geographic Regions. We examined how the reliability trends
varied across geographic regions. Based on the number of observations available, we were able
to divide the United States into four contiguous regions (details of this analysis are in Appendix
B). We found that the increase in the frequency with which reliability was addressed was fairly
widespread: the frequency rose after *Daubert* in all but one of the regions—the south region,
where it was already high before *Daubert*. There was some variation across regions in the timing
of the changes.

Differences Between Case Types. It appears that judges and challengers did not restrict
their attention to particular types of cases. Table 4.2 and Figure 4.2 show that while the patterns
were different, the frequency with which reliability was addressed rose at some point after
Daubert for all four of the case-type categories examined.[9] The frequency with which evidence
was addressed declined for one case-type category at the end of the period, and it may have
declined for others. The rougher time breakdown necessitated by the reduced number of
observations in each category may be hiding such an effect.

---

[9]The case types shown earlier, in Table 3.3, were combined into four categories to maintain an
adequate number of observations in each category. We ran separate regressions for each category. As in
the analysis of differences in challenges to defendants' versus plaintiffs' evidence, the regressions divided
the years into five time periods and the district courts into four geographic regions. Due to the smaller
number of observations, our results by case type are less precise than those based on the sample as a whole.

Table 4.2

**Proportion of Challenged Evidence in Which Reliability Addressed and
Proportion Found Unreliable, by Case Type
(predicted percent with substantive area of evidence and geographic region held constant)**

Case Type	N	1/80–6/89	7/89–6/93	7/93–6/95	7/95–6/97	7/97–6/99
A. Reliability Addressed						
Product liability and toxic torts	187	86	80	78	90	92
Other BI and PD	93	47	35	61**	64	81**
Business transactions	111	59	16	34	19	65**
Other	210	62	49	58	71**	54
B. Evidence Found Unreliable						
Product liability and toxic torts	187	61	52	25	65	54
Other BI and PD	93	39	51	49	66	74
Business transactions	111	2	2	32**	9	33**
Other	210	31**	6	18*	23**	20**

NOTE: Reference period used to calculate statistical significance of changes is shaded. A single asterisk (*) indicates that the difference from the reference period is statistically significant at 10 percent; a double asterisk (**) indicates that the difference from the reference period is statistically significant at 5 percent.

Difference Depending on When Case Was Filed. The *Daubert* decision applied to cases filed both before and after the opinion was issued. We checked to see whether district court judges did indeed scrutinize reliability more carefully for both types of cases. To do this, we compared the filing dates for opinions in which reliability was addressed with those for opinions in which it was not addressed. If cases filed before and after *Daubert* were equally affected, one would expect there to be no systematic difference in the filing dates for the two sets of evidence. The results of our analysis are presented in Appendix C. They suggest that evidence in cases filed pre-*Daubert* and evidence in cases filed post-*Daubert* were both subject to increased scrutiny.

Interpretation

We draw several inferences from the observed trends in the proportion of challenged evidence in which reliability was addressed, the success rate of challenges to reliability, and the proportion of challenged evidence found unreliable. First, the results shown above, in Figure 4.1, suggest that the standards for reliability tightened in the years after the *Daubert* decision. The success rate for challenges rose, encouraging an increase in the proportion of challenges that targeted reliability. The result was that the proportion of challenged evidence found unreliable rose through June 1997. By superseding *Frye*'s deference to general acceptance, *Daubert* could have relaxed the standards for reliability. But if this were the case, one would expect that, if

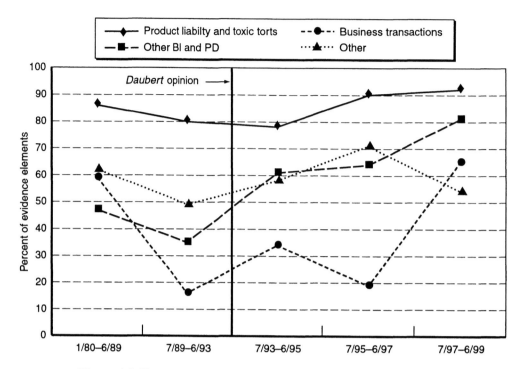

Figure 4.2–Frequency with Which Reliability Addressed, by Case Type (Substantive Area of Evidence and Geographic Region Held Constant)

anything, the success rate of challenges targeting reliability and the proportion of challenged evidence found unreliable would have fallen after *Daubert*, not risen.

The increase in the success rate of reliability challenges prior to June 1993 raises questions about whether *Daubert* caused the tightening of reliability standards. The increase may simply be a statistical fluke (the change between 7/89–6/91 and 7/91–6/93 is not statistically significant), or it may be driven by factors such as a change in the composition of the federal bench or a decline in the quality of evidence proposed prior to *Daubert*. In any event, the findings presented below on the types of evidence first affected after *Daubert* and the factors used by judges to assess reliability suggest that the decision was at least an important driver of the tightening of reliability standards after 1993.

While the evidence suggests that judges scrutinized the reliability of expert evidence more carefully after *Daubert*, two important caveats are necessary. First, our findings do not imply that this increased scrutiny resulted in better outcomes. As will be discussed in Section 8, outcomes improve only if standards are tightened in the right ways. Inappropriate or improperly applied standards may cause reliable evidence to be excluded and unreliable evidence to be admitted. Our analysis cannot determine whether the tighter standards were scientifically appropriate; that is a task for future study. Second, our findings provide only limited information on how widespread these changes were across the federal bench. The observation of similar effects in several different regions of the country and for different case types suggests that the changes in standards were not limited to a relatively small number of judges. However, additional data are needed to understand how widespread the changes were.

The second major inference we draw from the trends in Figure 4.1 is that proposers of evidence did not respond immediately to the increased reliability requirements by adjusting the quality of evidence proposed. If they had responded immediately, we would likely have seen little change in the proportion of evidence in which reliability was addressed, the success rate, or the proportion found unreliable. One likely reason for the gradual response is the difficulty or cost of improving the quality of evidence for cases already in the pipeline when requirements increased. Another likely reason is the initial uncertainty about whether the reliability requirements had tightened or relaxed.

Our third inference is that the declines in the proportion of challenged evidence in which reliability is addressed, the success rate, and the proportion of evidence found unreliable after July 1997 suggest that parties responded over time to the increased scrutiny given reliability. It may be that proposers adapted to the new standards, or that challengers increased the proportion of overall expert evidence they challenged on reliability grounds, or both. Our data do not allow us to distinguish among these hypotheses, but in any case, the findings do suggest that the parties responded to a tightening of standards.

There are a number of reasons why the frequency with which reliability is addressed, the success rate, and the proportion of evidence found unreliable could rise and then fall in the absence of any change in the reliability standards. While such factors may have played some role in the patterns observed during the 1990s, we believe they cannot fully account for the trends observed here. The rise and fall could be due to an unusual type of case that was working its way through the system. However, the observation of effects in different geographic regions and across different types of cases makes this unlikely. The pattern could also be due to a glut of low-quality evidence introduced soon after *Daubert* by proposers emboldened by a belief that standards for admitting evidence were less stringent. However, the increase in the proportion of evidence in which reliability was addressed and the increase in the proportion found unreliable following *Daubert* were due in part to increases for cases filed pre-*Daubert*, making this hypothesis doubtful. The decline in the proportion of evidence found unreliable could also have been caused by a gradual loosening of standards beginning in the late 1990s. Reports from practitioners and the legal literature provide no support for such an explanation.

The rise in the proportions reported in Figure 4.1 could also be explained by an *increase* in how often judges wrote their decisions when expert evidence was excluded relative to how often they wrote their decisions when challenged evidence was admitted. It may well be that judges are more likely to write opinions that exclude expert evidence than that admit it, and that the rates at which reliability is addressed and evidence found unreliable are higher in the opinions examined here than for challenges to expert evidence overall.[10] However, what matters for our analysis is whether there has been an *increase* over time in the rate at which decisions excluding evidence are written relative to the rate at which decisions admitting evidence are written. We see no compelling reason a priori for this to be the case. It seems just as plausible that a directive to examine reliability more carefully would induce judges to document their reasons for admitting evidence more fully. Moreover, it seems unlikely on empirical grounds that changes in the relative propensities to document evidence could explain the patterns observed here. The relative rate at which exclusions are written would have to rise and then for some reason fall to earlier levels. We observed in our analysis (see discussion below) a number of trends strongly suggesting that more is going on than a systematic increase and then decline in the relative frequency with which exclusions are written up. While we doubt that changes in this relative rate could explain the patterns we found, there are no direct data on the rates at which judges issue written opinions on challenges to expert evidence. Further investigation of this issue is warranted.

Finally, the rise could be explained by a simple change in terminology and no real change in whether a particular piece of evidence would be excluded or included. For example, judges may have increasingly expressed their objections to evidence in terms of reliability rather than relevance. We will return to this issue in Section 6, where we conclude that such a substitution could not account for all the changes observed.

4.2   HOW JUDGES INTERPRETED *DAUBERT'S* SCOPE

When the *Daubert* opinion was issued, there was uncertainty about whether it applied to expert evidence generally or only to "hard" science. *Daubert* addressed epidemiological evidence in a Bendectin case, and some argued that the decision applied only to scientific evidence narrowly defined. Others argued that it applied to all areas of expert evidence, including, for example, social and behavioral science and engineering. This issue was resolved by the Supreme Court's *Kumho* decision in December 1999, when the Court affirmed that the *Daubert* approach applied to all expert evidence. This section investigates how broadly judges applied *Daubert* prior to *Kumho*.

---

[10]A decision to admit evidence is not a final determination, and the court may consider documentation less necessary in this case than when evidence is excluded.

Table 4.3

**Proportion of Evidence in Which Reliability Addressed and Proportion Found Unreliable,
by Substantive Area of Evidence
(predicted percent with case type and geographic region held constant)**

		Opinion Date				
	N	1/80–6/89	7/89–6/93	7/93–6/95	7/95–6/97	7/97–6/99
A. Reliability Addressed						
Health care and medicine	107	58*	23	17	62**	62**
Engineering and technology	115	44	45	43	67	63
Physical science	92	93	83	97*	80	86
Social and behavioral science	97	80	56	61	89	84*
Business, law, and public administration	143	17	10	17	19	19
B. Evidence Found Unreliable						
Health care and medicine	107	34	14	9	31	25
Engineering and technology	115	32	24	9	46	20
Physical science	92	46	56	76	58	54
Social and behavioral science	97	43**	8	31*	61**	47**
Business, law, and public administration	143	5	1	11**	8*	14**

NOTE: Reference period used to calculate statistical significance of changes is shaded. A single asterisk (*) indicates that the difference from the reference period is statistically significant at 10 percent; a double asterisk (**) indicates that the difference from the reference period is statistically significant at 5 percent.

Findings

Table 4.3 reports trends in the frequency with which reliability was addressed and the proportion of evidence found unreliable in each of five different substantive areas (see Table 3.4 and the related discussion there). The trends control for changes in case type and in the geographic region in which the opinion was issued. Trends over time are also graphed in Figures 4.3 and 4.4 for easy evaluation. As in the analysis by case type, the reduced number of observations in each substantive area led us to divide the opinion dates into only five periods.[11]

All substantive areas of evidence showed increases in the proportion of evidence in which reliability was addressed and the proportion found unreliable. The proportions rose first for physical science, but there were later rises for health care and medicine; engineering and technology; social and behavioral science; and business, law, and public administration.

[11]A separate regression was run for each substantive area. Due to the smaller sample sizes, the federal court districts were collapsed into four contiguous regions and the case types were collapsed into four categories.

-34-

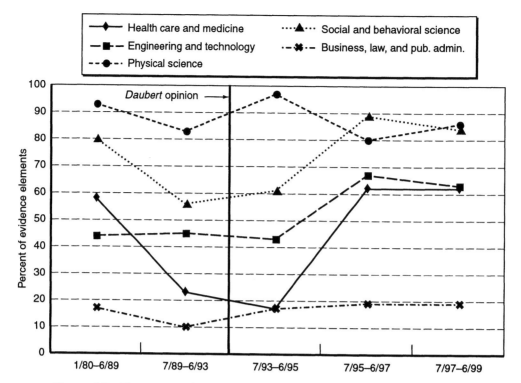

**Figure 4.3—Frequency with Which Reliability Addressed, by Substantive
Area of Evidence (Case Type and Geographic Region Held Constant)**

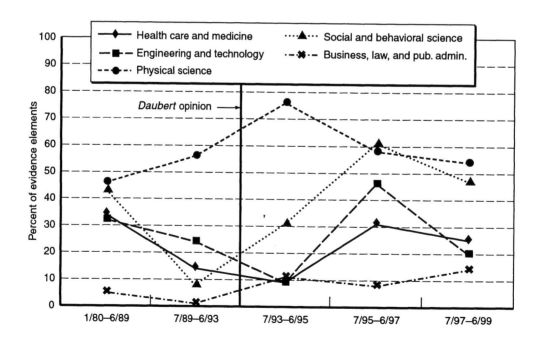

**Figure 4.4—Frequency with Which Evidence Found Unreliable, by Substantive
Area of Evidence (Case Type and Geographic Region Held Constant)**

Interpretation

The results suggest that challengers and judges initially focused on the type of evidence that the *Daubert* opinion addressed—evidence from the physical sciences. It appears, however, that over time challengers broadened their focus to include other types of expert evidence, and judges increasingly ruled such evidence unreliable. Thus, *Kumho* appears to have confirmed a trend already under way in federal district courts to apply Daubert broadly rather than restrict it to "hard" science.

These results also provide evidence as to what caused the changes in how often reliability was addressed and how often evidence was found unreliable. In Section 3, we discussed a number of possible explanations for changes in these outcomes, including changes in the Federal Rules of Evidence, changes in the composition of the federal bench, and the *Daubert* decision. The findings presented here reveal a signature that might be expected from the *Daubert* decision—an effect on evidence from the physical sciences first. This signature suggests that *Daubert* was at least an important part of the changes observed after June 1993.

5. TRENDS IN FACTORS ENTERING INTO THE RELIABLITY ASSESSMENT

This section delves into the factors judges use to evaluate whether evidence is reliable. We examine changes over time in the factors discussed in written opinions and in how challenged evidence measures up against these factors. We use the findings to make inferences about how judges are assessing reliability and the importance of general acceptance in their evaluations. Our findings suggest that judges are increasingly examining the clarity and coherence of an expert's explanation of the theory, method, and procedures underlying his or her findings and that general acceptance has, if anything, increased in importance since *Daubert*.

We start by defining the reliability factors used in our analysis. We then examine how often these factors are addressed in written opinions and how often challenged evidence falls short on each factor. We conclude by exploring how the importance of general acceptance has changed since *Daubert*.

5.1 FACTORS THAT ENTER INTO THE RELIABILITY ASSESSMENT

We assembled a list of factors that might be germane to assessing whether evidence is reliable. We based the list on reviews of federal district court, appellate, and Supreme Court opinions; law review articles; briefs written by scientific organizations for the *Daubert* case; and other books and articles on science in the courts.

Table 5.1 presents the list, along with some clarifying comments. The first five factors listed are those that the Supreme Court gave in the *Daubert* opinion as examples of factors judges should take into account when assessing reliability. The Court did not require, however, that these five factors be considered in every situation or prohibit other factors from being considered.

5.2 TRENDS IN RELIABILITY FACTORS

For each of the 601 elements of evidence in our sample, the coders recorded which reliability factors were discussed and whether the judge rated the evidence favorably, unfavorably, or neither favorably or unfavorably on each factor.[1] As before, the frequency with which a factor is addressed likely reflects challengers' decisions to challenge evidence on that basis. The proportion of evidence rated unfavorably on a factor reflects both the frequency with which the evidence is questioned on that factor and the standards applied by judges in evaluating the evidence on that factor.

---

[1]The coders were not required to find any particular wording or phrasing when determining whether a specific reliability factor was discussed. Rather, they were instructed to see whether the issue addressed by the factor was reflected somewhere in the discussion.

Table 5.1

Factors Potentially Entering into the Reliability Assessment

Factor	Comments and Examples
1. Peer review and publication	For example, publication of study results in scientific journals
2. General acceptance in relevant expert community	Need not be universal acceptance, but exact requirement is vague
3. Potential for testing or actual testing	Has the theory been tested? Can it in principle ever be tested?
4. Known or potential rate of error	How often does a test, or procedure, produce incorrect results?
5. Existence and maintenance of standards controlling use of technique or method	Were samples properly collected? Were instruments properly calibrated?
6. Clarity and coherence of expert's explanation of theory, methods, and procedures	Does the expert openly describe how analysis was done? Does reasoning hang together logically?
7. Proper extrapolation	Can results of an animal study be extrapolated to humans?
8. Breadth of facts, data, or studies underlying analysis	Are conclusions based on more than anecdotes? Are they based on multiple studies?
9. Reliance on verifiable evidence or data	Can data be checked?
10. Control for or consideration of confounding factors	Were other possible causes of an injury or condition considered? Was an adequate control used?
11. Use of facts or data reasonably relied on by experts in field	Is expert following standard practice in field?
12. Consistency of theory or findings with other studies, principles, or experts in field	Are components of a new theory consistent with what is already known?
13. Statistical significance of findings	—
14. Existence of real-world data to support theory	Is there evidence outside laboratory tests that, e.g., substance actually causes cancer?
15. Court-appointed neutral expert's evaluation of evidence	—
16. Purpose for which research was conducted	Was the research done for purposes of litigation?
17. Reputation of expert	Is expert well thought of in his/her field?

Findings

Table 5.2 reports trends over time in how often the reliability factors are addressed and how often the evidence is rated unfavorably on each factor. As in other analyses, we held case type, substantive area of evidence, and geographic region constant.[2] Recall that the predicted levels in Table 5.2 would be different if a different combination of case type, substantive area of evidence, and region were used as reference categories, but that the trends over time would be

---

[2]Even though the analysis for each factor was done on all 601 elements of evidence, we broke time into five periods rather than the eight used to analyze reliability overall (see Subsection 4.1). This was necessary because the frequency with which an individual reliability factor was addressed is much lower than the frequency with which reliability overall was addressed. For the same reason, we collapsed the appellate circuits into four regions and the different case types into four categories in the statistical analysis.

Table 5.2

Proportion of Evidence Elements in Which Reliability Factors Addressed and Proportion Rated Unfavorably
(predicted percent with case type, substantive area of evidence, and geographic region held constant)

Reliability Factors	1/80–6/89	7/89–6/93	7/93–6/95	7/95–6/97	7/97–6/99
A. Factor Addressed					
1. Peer review and publication	13	13	19	37**	24
2. General acceptance in relevant expert community	13	9	16	28**	25**
3. Potential for testing or actual testing	8	6	18	39**	14
4. Known or potential rate of error	16	3	21	28**	16
5. Existence and maintenance of standards controlling use of technique or method	12	3	29**	36**	16
6. Clarity and coherence of expert's explanation of theory, methods, and procedures	26	13	17	35**	48**
7. Proper extrapolation	19	16	15	18	25
8. Breadth of facts, data, or studies underlying analysis	27	21	20	18	21
9. Reliance on verifiable evidence or data	25**	8	14	18*	20**
10. Control for or consideration of confounding factors	14	8	17	17	21*
B. Factor Rated Unfavorably					
1. Peer review and publication	7	7	6	34**	10
2. General acceptance in relevant expert community	15	10	4	32**	16
3. Potential for testing or actual testing	4	3	12	33**	10
4. Known or potential rate of error	12	4	14	22*	13
5. Existence and maintenance of standards controlling use of technique or method	8	3	23**	14	18
6. Clarity and coherence of expert's explanation of theory, methods, and procedures	19	10	16	31**	49**
7. Proper extrapolation	9	12	14	14	23
8. Breadth of facts, data, or studies underlying analysis	17**	7	5	10	10
9. Reliance on verifiable evidence or data	18*	6	13	16*	20**
10. Control for or consideration of confounding factors	19	9	23	18	21

NOTE: Reference period used to calculate statistical significance of changes is shaded. A single asterisk (*) indicates that the difference from the reference period is statistically significant at 10 percent; a double asterisk (**) indicates that the difference from the reference period is statistically significant at 5 percent.

similar. Raw data (i.e., unadjusted for changes in case type, substantive area of evidence, and region) on the frequencies with which the reliability factors are addressed and the evidence is rated unfavorably are reported in Table A.8 of Appendix A.

In both panels of Table 5.2, the five *Daubert* factors are listed above the dashed line and the five most commonly addressed non-*Daubert* factors are listed below it (see full set of 17 factors in Table 5.1). The remaining seven factors were rarely mentioned in the opinions we examined and are not included in Table 5.2. The statistical significance of the difference from the level observed during the two years prior to *Daubert* is noted. The results are presented graphically in Figures 5.1 and 5.2.

All five *Daubert* factors were addressed more frequently after *Daubert*. Panel A of Table 5.2 and Figure 5.1a show that while the *Daubert* factors were sometimes addressed even before the decision, the post-*Daubert* increases were both substantial and statistically significant.[3] As was the case for reliability more generally (see Figure 4.1), the frequency with which the *Daubert* factors were addressed fell at the end of the period. Two of the *Daubert* factors—general acceptance and peer review and publication—remained at higher levels than the other three at the end of the period. Panel B of Table 5.2 and Figure 5.1b show that the proportion of evidence rated unfavorably on each *Daubert* factor also rose after the decision but then eventually fell.

There were also increases in the frequencies with which most of the non-*Daubert* factors were addressed and the evidence rated unfavorably on each. The increases for the clarity and coherence of the expert's explanation are particularly striking (see Figures 5.2a and 5.2b). And in contrast to the results for all but one of the *Daubert* factors, the frequencies with which the non-*Daubert* factors were addressed and the evidence rated unfavorably did not decline at the end of the period.

Interpretation

The data suggest that after *Daubert*, challengers and judges initially focused on the *Daubert* factors when, respectively, challenging and evaluating reliability, but that they then paid increasing attention to other reliability factors over time. There is a sensible explanation for this pattern. Initially, many judges were probably learning how to evaluate reliability and were uncertain about the latitude they had in their investigation. Under such circumstances, the most prudent action for judges and challengers alike would be to stick closely to the *Daubert* factors. As time passed, however, judges gained experience in evaluating reliability, and appellate court

---

[3]Groscup et al. (2000) found no increase in the number of words on the *Daubert* factors in federal and state appellate court decisions on criminal cases after *Daubert*. This may reflect differences between the issues addressed by appellate and trial court judges or differences between civil and criminal cases.

opinions clarified their authority. Judges and challengers then felt less compelled to address each *Daubert* factor and paid increasing attention to more-general factors important to assessing reliability.[4]

Judges and challengers increasingly focused on the clarity and coherence of the expert's explanation of the underlying theory, methods, and procedures. The increases in the frequencies with which this factor was addressed and the evidence rated unfavorably on it suggest that judges continued to evaluate the theory, methods, and procedures underlying expert evidence even after attention to the *Daubert* factors waned.

Our findings, like those on differences in the frequency with which reliability was addressed by substantive area of evidence (see Subsection 4.2) again provide evidence that the *Daubert* decision was at least partly responsible for the changes in the second half of the 1990s. The peaks in the frequencies with which the *Daubert* factors were addressed and the evidence was rated unfavorably on each correspond to the peaks in the frequencies with which reliability was addressed and the evidence was found unreliable.

5.3 ROLE OF GENERAL ACCEPTANCE

The role that general acceptance should play in a judge's decision to exclude expert evidence was at the heart of the *Daubert* decision, and we here evaluate how this role has changed over time. It is not obvious how *Daubert* might have affected the importance placed on general acceptance. First, as discussed in Subsection 1.1, there is uncertainty about the role of general acceptance before *Daubert*. Second, there is uncertainty a priori about the emphasis judges would place on general acceptance after *Daubert*. On the one hand, even though general acceptance is one of the *Daubert* factors, an increasing focus on direct examination of the method underlying the evidence may limit general acceptance's importance. On the other, general acceptance may be used by judges as a convenient indicator of reliability and be critical to admissibility.[5]

Table 5.3 provides a first cut at how the importance of general acceptance has changed over time. The table reports the percentage of evidence found unreliable in four different circumstances: (1) when the judge rated the evidence favorably on general acceptance, (2) when

---

[4]It may also be that parties proposing evidence learned how to package it in ways that satisfied the *Daubert* factors.

[5]The survey of state trial court judges conducted by Gatowski et al. (2001, p. 448) found little consensus on the relative importance of the *Daubert* criteria. However, there was some indication that general acceptance would be given the most weight. On a question concerning which *Daubert* factor they would weight the most heavily, over one-half of the judges answering the question indicated general acceptance, which was far more than the proportion indicating any other *Daubert* factor.

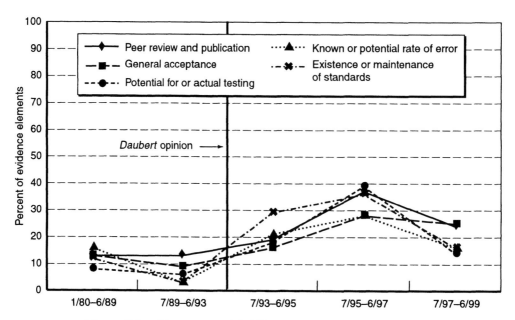

**Figure 5.1a—Frequency with Which *Daubert* Factors Addressed
(Case Type, Substantive Area of Evidence, and Geographic Region
Held Constant)**

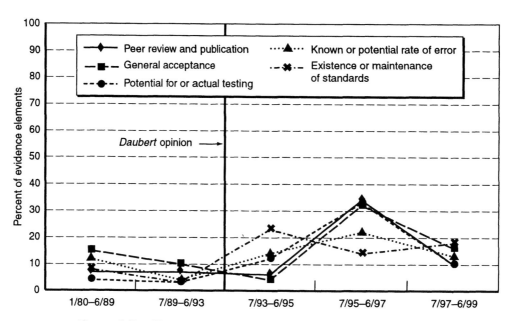

**Figure 5.1b—Frequency with Which Evidence Rated Unfavorably on
Daubert Factors (Case Type, Substantive Area of Evidence,
and Geographic Region Held Constant)**

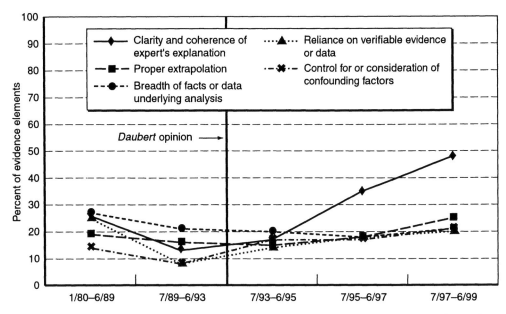

Figure 5.2a—Frequency with Which Other Reliability Factors Addressed (Case Type, Substantive Area of Evidence, and Geographic Region Held Constant)

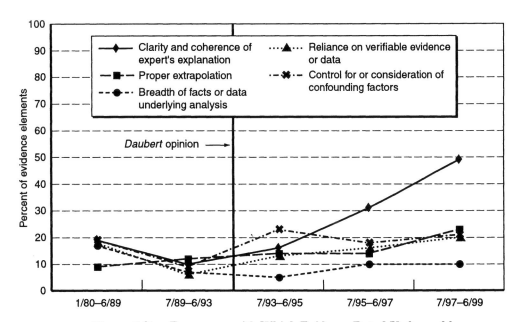

Figure 5.2b—Frequency with Which Evidence Rated Unfavorably on Other Reliability Factors (Case Type, Substantive Area of Evidence, and Geographic Region Held Constant)

Table 5.3

**Decisiveness of General Acceptance: Percentage of Evidence Found
Unreliable for Different General Acceptance Ratings**

Rating on General Acceptance	1/80–6/93		7/93–6/99	
	N	Percent Rated Unreliable	N	Percent Rated Unreliable
Favorable	4	0	20	10
Neutral	0	—	3	0
Unfavorable	8	88	27	96
Not addressed	214	18	325	25
Total	226	20	375	29

the judge addressed general acceptance but rated the evidence neither favorably nor unfavorably on general acceptance, (3) when the judge rated the evidence unfavorably on general acceptance, and (4) when the judge did not address general acceptance. The table compares the decisiveness of general acceptance—i.e., the relation between the rating on general acceptance and the probability that evidence is excluded—only pre- and post-*Daubert*, because the limited number of times that general acceptance was addressed in our data prevented a more detailed analysis.

Several observations about the results in Table 5.3 are noteworthy. First, general acceptance was seldom addressed before *Daubert*—it was addressed for only 12 of the 226 elements of evidence (5 percent). How rarely it was addressed suggests that general acceptance was not a commonly used standard for determining reliability. Second, pre-*Daubert*, whenever challenged evidence was found to be generally accepted, it was rated reliable. After *Daubert*, 10 percent of evidence found to be generally accepted was rated unreliable. Although the pre-*Daubert* sample size is small, the findings suggest that general acceptance was a sufficient condition for reliability pre- but not post-*Daubert*. After *Daubert*, evidence could be generally accepted but still not rated reliable. Third, evidence found to be not generally accepted was, if anything, more likely to be rated unreliable after *Daubert* than before. Of eight elements of evidence rated unfavorably on general acceptance through June 1993, seven were found unreliable (88 percent). After June 1993, 26 of 27 elements rated unfavorably on general acceptance were found unreliable (96 percent).

We repeated this analysis of the importance of general acceptance for the proportion of challenged evidence excluded (see Appendix D). The results are similar to those reported in Table 5.3 but, if anything, provide more-convincing evidence that general acceptance was not sufficient for getting expert evidence admitted after *Daubert*.

The conclusions we can draw from Table 5.3 are limited given that evidence rated unfavorably on general acceptance is frequently rated unfavorably on other reliability factors as well. For example, evidence found not generally accepted might also have problems with regard to its underlying method. What we would really like to know is how often evidence is found unreliable when it is rated unfavorably solely on general acceptance.

To provide insight into this question, we used a regression framework that examines the importance of one factor while holding other factors constant (see Appendix D). When ratings on other reliability factors were held constant, we found that general acceptance was a good post-*Daubert* predictor of whether evidence was found unreliable. In contrast, general acceptance was not a good predictor prior to *Daubert*. The number of times evidence was found not generally accepted before *Daubert* is small, and the statistical precision of our estimates is low. However, the results support the suggestion from Table 5.3 that evidence found not to be generally accepted was, if anything, more likely to be found unreliable after *Daubert* than before.[6]

_____

[6]We also repeated the regression analysis using whether or not the evidence was excluded as the outcome variable. The results were similar (see Appendix D).

6. TRENDS IN THE OTHER CRITERIA USED TO ASSESS EXPERT EVIDENCE

So far we have focused on the reliability of expert evidence. We have examined trends in how often reliability is addressed, how often evidence is found unreliable, and what factors enter into the reliability assessment. Now we turn to the other criteria judges use to assess expert evidence: relevance, qualifications, and other considerations. Data on trends in these criteria allow us to explore whether judges have scrutinized reliability more carefully since *Daubert* or whether there has been nothing more than a switch in terminology. We conclude that while parties challenging evidence may have recast some challenges in terms of reliability since *Daubert*, there has not merely been a shift in terminology.

We begin by reviewing the definitions of the various criteria and discussing how challenges directed at one criterion may be recast as challenges directed at reliability. We then examine trends in the assessment of relevance, qualifications, and other considerations over time and interpret the findings.

6.1 RECASTING CHALLENGES TO EXPERT EVIDENCE AS CHALLENGES BASED ON RELIABILITY

As discussed in Subsection 2.1, three major criteria enter into federal district court judges' decisions on whether to admit evidence: reliability, relevance, and qualifications. Judges also take other considerations into account, such as whether the evidence is unfairly prejudicial or is based on privileged information. In many cases, the distinctions between these criteria are blurry.

Relevance refers to whether the evidence will assist the trier of fact in determining a fact at issue. It is often difficult to distinguish an objection based on relevance from an objection based on reliability. For example, consider testimony that asserts a substance causes cancer in humans based on the results of animal studies. Such testimony might be considered unreliable because it is based on research that cannot be reliably extrapolated to humans. But it might instead be considered irrelevant because the research sheds no light on whether the substance causes cancer in humans.

Qualifications refers to whether the expert has specialized knowledge in the field relevant to the testimony. It is easy to imagine how a party challenging an expert's qualifications could recast such a challenge in terms of reliability. For example, instead of arguing that the expert does not have the proper training to present evidence on a certain topic, the challenger could argue that the expert's testimony is unreliable because he or she has inadequate knowledge of the methods in the field.

6.2 TRENDS IN RELEVANCE, QUALIFICATIONS, AND OTHER CONSIDERATIONS

We recorded whether judges addressed relevance,[1] qualifications,[2] and other considerations in their opinions and whether they rated the evidence favorably, unfavorably, or neither on each criterion.

Findings

Overall, we found that relevance was addressed only slightly less frequently than reliability (42 percent of the 601 elements of evidence for relevance versus 48 percent for reliability—see Table A.7 in Appendix A). The success rate for challenges based on relevance was similar to that for challenges based on reliability (54 percent versus 53 percent), meaning that, as with reliability, roughly one-quarter of the evidence was rated unfavorably. In comparison, qualifications and other considerations were addressed less often, and the success rates for challenges were lower, with the result that less than 10 percent of the evidence in our sample was rated unfavorably for each of these two criteria.

Panel A of Table 6.1 first reports trends in the frequency with which each criterion was addressed. These trends hold case type, substantive area of evidence, and appellate circuit in which the district court lies constant.[3] Panel B reports trends in the success rates of the challenges on each criterion; Panel C reports how the frequency of unfavorable ratings changed over time. Figures 6.1 through 6.4 display the results graphically. Keep in mind that the relative positions of the trend lines (e.g., the general level of the reliability trends relative to the relevance trends) depend on the particular case type, substantive area of evidence, and appellate circuit chosen to illustrate the regression results.[4] However, the trends over time for a given criterion would be similar if other reference categories were chosen.

---

[1]Coders marked an opinion as addressing relevance if the judge discussed whether the theory, methods, or findings of the expert evidence were related to the facts of the case. Coders also included as addressing relevance discussions on whether the expert was addressing issues that the jury should assess itself.

[2]Opinions were coded as addressing qualifications only if there was some indication that the judge actually evaluated the expert's qualifications. Simply describing an expert's background—e.g., "Dr. Jones has 15 years as a toxicologist"—was not enough. Statements such as, "Although Dr. Jones is not an M.D., he is an experienced toxicologist," were taken as evidence that the judge was evaluating the expert's qualifications.

[3]Time is broken into five periods rather than the eight used in other parts of our analysis because the sample sizes for the success rates are relatively small and because the frequencies with which relevance, qualifications, and other considerations are addressed are less than the frequency with which reliability is addressed. The logit models use the same breakdowns for case type, substantive area of evidence, and appellate circuit as the models used for Table 4.1, however.

[4]As in earlier sections, predictions are made for a product liability case, evidence from the physical sciences, and a district in the Third Appellate Circuit.

Table 6.1

Trends in Frequencies with Which Different Criteria Addressed and Evidence Rated Unfavorably on Each Criterion
(predicted percent with case type, substantive area of evidence, and appellate circuit held constant)

Opinion Date	Criterion			
	Reliability	Relevance	Qualifications	Other Considerations
A. Criterion Addressed (N=601)				
1/80-6/89	79*	14	27	21
7/89-6/93	68	15	20	14
7/93-6/95	74	8**	20	15
7/95-6/97	84**	19	23	10
7/97-6/99	90**	7**	28	9
B. Evidence Rated Unfavorably on Criterion Given Criterion Addressed				
	(N=290)	(N=251)	(N=188)	(N=119)
1/80-6/89	67	32	19	13*
7/89-6/93	53	27	14	2
7/93-6/95	68	39	19	11*
7/95-6/97	71*	44	23	22**
7/97-6/99	64	23	13	6
C. Evidence Rated Unfavorably on Criterion (N=601)				
1/80-6/89	56**	7	5	1.8**
7/89-6/93	36	7	3	0.3
7/93-6/95	49	5	4	1.1**
7/95-6/97	62**	11	4	1.2**
7/97-6/99	58**	4**	3	<1

NOTE: Reference period used to calculate statistical significance of changes is shaded. A single asterisk (*) indicates that the difference from the reference period is statistically significant at 10 percent; a double asterisk (**) indicates that the difference from the reference period is statistically significant at 5 percent.

The frequencies with which reliability, relevance, and qualifications were addressed all rose, at least initially, after *Daubert*.[5] The frequency with which other considerations were addressed fell over time, but the decline is not statistically significant, and the magnitude of the decline since *Daubert* (5 percentage points) is smaller than the percentage point increase for reliability since *Daubert* (22 percentage points).

Although in many cases the changes are not statistically significant, Table 6.1 suggests that changes over time in the success rates for challenges directed at the different criteria were similar. All rose after *Daubert* and then trailed off at the end of the period.

---

[5]Figure 6.1 repeats the trends reported in Section 4 for the frequency with which reliability was addressed and the proportion of challenged evidence found unreliable. This time, however, there is no downturn in the frequency with which reliability was addressed at the end of the period because time is broken into fewer periods.

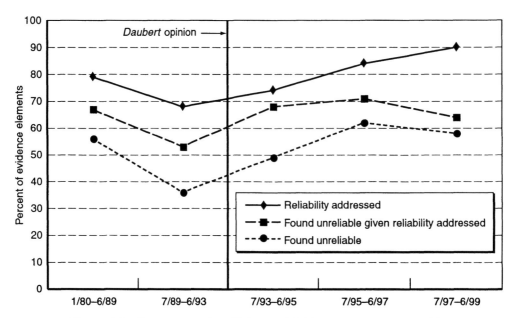

Figure 6.1—Frequency with Which Reliability Addressed and Evidence
Found Unreliable (Case Type, Substantive Area of Evidence, and
Appellate Circuit Held Constant)

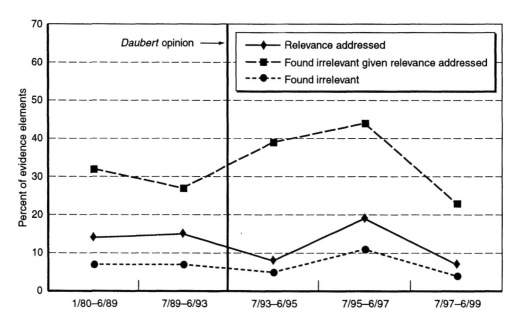

Figure 6.2—Frequency with Which Relevance Addressed and Evidence
Found Irrelevant (Case Type, Substantive Area of Evidence, and
Appellate Circuit Held Constant)

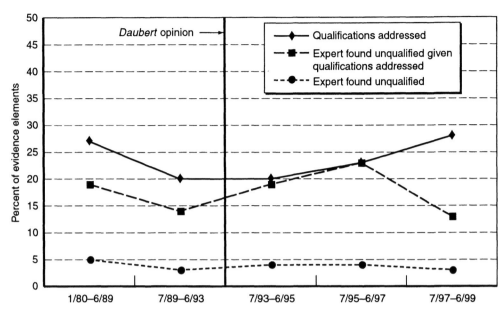

Figure 6.3—Frequency with Which Expert Qualifications Addressed and Expert Found Unqualified (Case Type, Substantive Area of Evidence, and Appellate Circuit Held Constant)

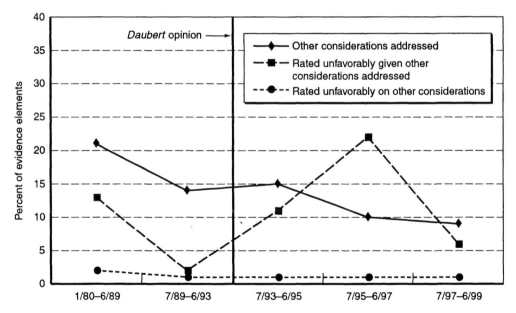

Figure 6.4—Frequency with Which Other Considerations Addressed and Evidence Rated Unfavorably on Other Considerations (Case Type, Substantive Area of Evidence, and Appellate Circuit Held Constant)

For three of the four criteria, the frequency with which evidence was rated unfavorably rose after *Daubert* and then fell at the end of the period. (The changes for the other considerations cannot be seen in Figure 6.4 because the overall level is so low.) There was little change over time in the frequency with which experts were found unqualified.

As in the case of reliability, we were not able to detect much difference between plaintiffs and defendants in the trends for the other criteria. The frequency with which relevance was addressed rose and then fell for both plaintiffs and defendants after *Daubert*, although the changes were not statistically significant because of the modest sample size. For neither group was there much change in the frequency with which qualifications were addressed, and the frequency with which other criteria were addressed was too low to detect differences between plaintiffs and defendants over time.

Interpretation

Our results on changes in the various criteria addressed and evidence rated unfavorably suggest that there was an increase in judicial scrutiny of reliability, not merely a shift in terminology from relevance, qualifications, and other considerations to reliability. If a simple substitution of reliability for relevance had occurred, the frequency with which relevance was addressed should have moved in the opposite direction of that for reliability. If challengers had increasingly challenged reliability instead of qualifications, one would expect the frequency with which qualifications were addressed to fall over the period. We did not see either pattern. The frequency with which other considerations were addressed does trail off after *Daubert*, but as discussed above, the declines were not statistically significant and not large in magnitude. What is more, as we will see in Section 7, the proportion of challenged evidence excluded rose after *Daubert*, providing strong evidence that *Daubert* induced more than a shift in terminology.

The findings also suggest that judges started evaluating evidence more critically in terms of all criteria, not just reliability. The increased success rates for challenges directed at the various criteria are not all statistically significant, but they do suggest that once judges became more-watchful gatekeepers, they looked more carefully not only at reliability, but at relevance, qualifications, and other considerations as well.

7. CONSEQUENCES OF MORE-WATCHFUL GATEKEEPING

The previous three sections describe indications we found that judges have become more-watchful gatekeepers for expert evidence since *Daubert*. These findings suggest that standards for reliability have tightened and that judges have examined challenged evidence more carefully with respect to other criteria as well. This section examines some of the consequences of this enhanced scrutiny. We first examine its effect on the proportion of challenged evidence excluded; we then examine its effect on one possible outcome when evidence is excluded—summary judgment. Finally, we examine changes in the types of evidence challenged.

7.1   TRENDS IN PROPORTION OF CHALLENGED EVIDENCE EXCLUDED

Findings

Table 7.1 shows the proportion of challenged expert evidence excluded when the evidence is found lacking in terms of reliability, relevance, qualifications, or other considerations. As can be seen, evidence rated negatively on any one of these criteria is almost always excluded, both prior to and after *Daubert*. Trends in the proportion of challenged evidence found lacking on the basis of one or more criteria thus closely mirror trends in the proportion of challenged evidence excluded.

Table 7.2 shows that slightly over one-half of the 601 challenged elements of evidence in our sample were excluded overall (see Raw Data columns).[1] When case type, substantive area of evidence, and appellate circuit are held constant, the proportion of challenged evidence rises after *Daubert* and then falls (see last column of Table 7.2 and see Figure 7.1).[2] The pattern mirrors the patterns for the proportion of evidence found unreliable (see Table 4.1) and for the proportions of evidence rated unfavorably on relevance and on expert qualifications (see Table 6.1).

---

[1]If judges write opinions more frequently when evidence is excluded than when it is admitted, the proportion of all challenged evidence that is excluded will be less than the proportion reported here. (Data on the frequencies with which exclusions and admissions of evidence are written are not available.) What is important for our analysis, however, is whether the frequency with which exclusions were written changed relative to the frequency with which admissions were written. For reasons discussed in Subsection 4.1, we doubt that such a change could explain the patterns we observed.

[2]Our findings are consistent with those of Johnson, Krafka, and Cecil (2000) but inconsistent with those of Groscup et al. (2000). The latter study found no change in the exclusion rate post-*Daubert*, which may be due in part to differences between trial court and appellate court decisions and between civil and criminal cases.

Table 7.1

Percentage of Time Evidence Excluded When Rated Unfavorably on the Different Criteria

Criterion on Which Evidence Rated Unfavorably	1/80–6/93		7/93–6/99	
	N	Percent Excluded	N	Percent Excluded
Reliability	46	98	108	99
Relevance	56	100	81	98
Qualifications	21	100	35	94
Other considerations	16	100	27	96

Table 7.2

Percentage of Challenged Evidence Excluded

Opinion Date	Raw Data		Predicted Percent Excluded When Case Type, Substantive Area, and Appellate Circuit Held Constant
	N	Percent Excluded	
1/80–6/89	93	52	50
7/89–6/91	55	45	44
7/91–6/93	78	55	53
7/93–6/95	106	46	45
7/95–6/96	78	64	61
7/96–6/97	65	71	70*
7/97–6/98	62	46	44
7/98–6/99	64	44	46
All periods	601	53	—

NOTE: Reference period used to calculate statistical significance of changes is shaded. The single asterisk (*) indicates that the difference from the reference period is statistically significant at 10 percent.

Our data on challenges to defendants' evidence are limited, but they suggest that the patterns for challenges to plaintiffs' evidence and to defendants' evidence were similar. As expected, we found that the proportion of plaintiffs' evidence excluded closely resembled that in Figure 7.1. The proportion of defendants' evidence excluded peaked at the same time, but due to the small sample size, the difference from the reference period was not statistically significant.

Interpretation

The rise in the proportion of challenged evidence excluded after *Daubert* provides further evidence that post-*Daubert* changes in standards for admitting expert evidence were more than just shifts in terminology. These changes had real impacts on the proportion of expert evidence excluded.

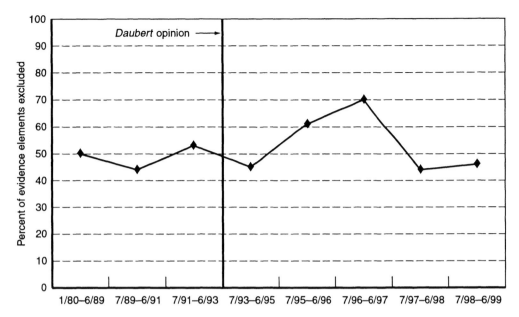

Figure 7.1—Percentage of Evidence Elements Excluded (Case Type, Substantive Area of Evidence, and Appellate Circuit Held Constant)

A rise in the proportion of evidence excluded provides incentives to both plaintiffs and defendants to change their behavior. Higher exclusion rates presumably induce plaintiffs to change the nature of evidence they propose; higher success rates presumably encourage defendants to challenge more evidence. Both responses will tend to reduce the exclusion rate—as observed in Figure 7.1.

7.2 TRENDS IN SUMMARY JUDGMENT

The exclusion of expert evidence can have a number of different consequences. Exclusion of plaintiffs' evidence may lead plaintiffs to narrow the case, drop the case altogether, or accept a reduced settlement. Exclusion of defendants' evidence may lead defendants to accept certain allegations by plaintiffs and may lead to settlement.[3] Exclusion may also lead to summary judgment. In summary judgment, the judge makes a decision on some or all of the issues in the case. Parties challenging evidence may request summary judgment based on the exclusion of evidence. For example, defendants challenging plaintiffs' evidence may argue that the plaintiffs' case has no basis in the absence of the challenged evidence and request that the judge throw out the case if the evidence is excluded. Summary judgment may resolve the entire case, as in this example, or be partial, resolving only some issues.

---

[3]For example, defendants may no longer contest that their actions caused an injury, leaving only the amount of damages to be resolved.

The only information contained in written opinions on the consequences of excluding expert evidence is whether summary judgment was granted. In the opinions we reviewed, we noted whether summary judgment was requested and whether it was granted based (at least partly) on exclusion of the challenged evidence. We found that summary judgment was requested in about one-third of challenges and was granted roughly one-half the time it was requested (see Table A.9 in Appendix A). The vast majority—88 percent—of the summary judgment requests in our sample were made in challenges to evidence proposed by plaintiffs; only 10 percent were made in challenges to defendants' evidence.[4] One-half of the summary judgment requests in our sample were linked to expert evidence on the cause of an injury or condition.

Table 7.3 shows the trends in summary judgment over time when case type, substantive area of evidence, and appellate circuit are held constant. Note, once again, that the overall level of the trend depends on the particular case type, substantive area, and circuit chosen as reference categories, but that the trend over time would be similar if other reference categories were chosen. The results demonstrate that the frequency with which summary judgment was requested rose substantially after *Daubert*, as did the frequency with which summary judgment was granted. This latter rise tailed off at the end of the period, whereas the former continued, implying that the success rate of summary judgment requests fell at the end of the period.

The trends in Table 7.3 show that challenges to expert evidence increasingly resulted in summary judgments. Because we think it unlikely that the proportion of summary judgments resulting in case dismissal (as opposed to resolution of some of the issues in the case—i.e., partial summary judgment) has fallen over time, we think it likely that challenges to plaintiffs' evidence have increasingly resulted in case dismissals.[5]

The increase in the frequency with which summary judgment was granted was driven partly by the increase in the frequency with which summary judgment was requested (the other factor being the success rate of the requests). This increased frequency of requests may be due partly to *Daubert*, but it may be driven by broader trends in litigation practices that have nothing to do with *Daubert*. For example, judges may have become more receptive to summary judgment

---

[4]The party proposing the evidence could not be identified in the remaining 2 percent.

[5]In extracting information from the opinions, we did not record whether a summary judgment resulted in case dismissal. However, we have no reason to think that the proportion of summary judgments that resulted in dismissal fell over time. The proportion of summary judgment requests that were made in conjunction with challenges to plaintiffs' evidence did not change over time (see Table A.9), and we would expect that, if anything, the proportion of these resulting in dismissal would rise, not fall. If the proportion of summary judgments resulting in dismissal did not fall over time, the increase in the proportion of challenges resulting in summary judgment means that the proportion of challenges resulting in dismissal increased as well.

Table 7.3

**Frequency with Which Summary Judgment Requested and
Granted When Evidence Challenged (Case Type, Substantive
Area of Evidence, and Appellate Circuit Held Constant)
(N=601 elements of evidence)**

Opinion Date	Summary Judgment Requested	Summary Judgment Granted
1/80–6/89	49	37
7/89–6/93	43	21
7/93–6/95	37	25
7/95–6/97	65**	48*
7/97–6/99	73**	42*

NOTE: Reference period used to calculate statistical significance of changes is shaded. A single asterisk (*) indicates that the difference from the reference period is statistically significant at 10 percent; a double asterisk (**) indicates that the difference from the reference period is statistically significant at 5 percent.

requests in an attempt to resolve cases more quickly and at lower cost. But *Daubert* may have led challengers to expand the scope of their challenges to the point where they increasingly challenged the entire basis of the case and thus more frequently requested summary judgment.

Summary judgment requests related to the exclusion of evidence may have in part increased due to a shift in the grounds on which dismissals are requested. For example, had standards for admitting evidence not tightened, defendants might have requested that the case be dismissed because the evidence was insufficient rather than inadmissible.[6] But such a shift, even if it did occur, does not mean that the standards for admitting expert evidence have not changed. What it may mean is that stricter standards for admitting evidence have not changed the ultimate outcome of many cases—i.e., cases dismissed after *Daubert* because expert evidence was excluded might have been dismissed on insufficiency grounds even if there had been no change in the standards. Additional data are needed to better understand what the increase in summary judgment based on the exclusion of evidence has meant to ultimate case outcomes.

7.3 TRENDS IN TYPE OF EVIDENCE CHALLENGED

So far we have examined trends in the outcomes of interest—such as proportion of challenged evidence found unreliable and proportion of challenged evidence excluded—while holding case type, substantive area of evidence, and appellate circuit constant. *Daubert* may also

---

[6]Legal researchers have observed that before *Daubert*, plaintiffs' cases were often unsuccessful not because judges refused to admit their proffered expert evidence, but because trial and appellate courts found that evidence insufficient even when plaintiffs received a jury verdict at trial (Margaret Berger, personal communication, June 2001).

have affected the mix of case types and substantive areas of evidence, so we now examine how both of these have changed over time.

As discussed in Subsection 2.4, the effect of stricter liability standards on the breakdown of challenged evidence by either case type or substantive area is indeterminant. On the one hand, parties may propose less of the types of evidence that fare poorly under *Daubert*, decreasing their share of all evidence challenged. On the other, parties may more aggressively challenge these types of evidence, increasing their share of all evidence challenged.

We did not find any noteworthy change in the mix of challenged evidence by case type (see Table A.1 in Appendix A). The proportion of opinions on challenged evidence that came from product liability cases rose somewhat at the end of the period, as did the proportion that came from employee relations cases. Both of these increases mirrored increases in the proportion of all federal civil cases that were product liability and employee relations cases (see Table A.2 in Appendix A).

Changes in the mix of challenged evidence by substantive area are more noteworthy. Figure 7.2 shows that evidence based on physical science constituted a higher share of the challenged evidence during the first three years after *Daubert* but a declining share in subsequent years.[7] The focus appears to have shifted to evidence based on engineering and technology and on health care and medicine. The increases in the shares of challenged evidence that were in

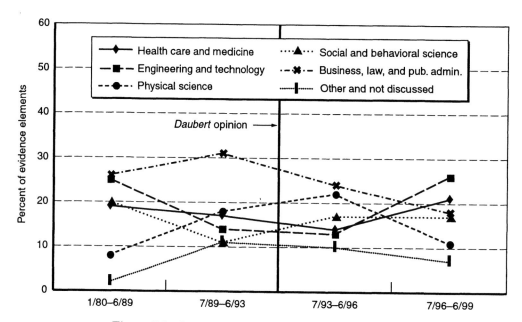

Figure 7.2—Mix of Challenged Evidence by Substantive Area

---

[7]The percentages in Figure 7.2 are based on the 601 elements of evidence. They are not adjusted for case type or appellate circuit.

these two substantive areas track those in the proportions of evidence for which reliability was addressed in these two areas over the period (see Figure 4.3). The results suggest that challenges initially focused on physical science and then moved to other areas. This may have come about because the quality of evidence based on physical science improved due to increased scrutiny. It may also have come about because *Daubert*'s applicability to all expert evidence, rather than just evidence from the physical sciences, became better established over time.

8. CONCLUSIONS AND NEXT STEPS

This report describes our analysis of written federal district court opinions, an analysis carried out to provide insight into how judges evaluate and screen expert evidence in the wake of the Supreme Court's 1993 *Daubert* decision. The findings are based on systematic coding of a substantial number of district court opinions between 1980 and 1999 and statistical analysis of the results. In this concluding section, we summarize our key findings and the conclusions we draw from them. We also identify important gaps that remain in understanding how judges screen expert evidence, as well as research that would help fill those gaps.

8.1 SUMMARY OF KEY CONCLUSIONS

After *Daubert*, Judges Scrutinized Reliability More Carefully and Applied Stricter Standards

Our analysis of district court opinions suggests that following *Daubert*, judges scrutinized reliability more carefully and applied stricter standards in deciding whether to admit expert evidence. After *Daubert*, the proportion of challenged evidence in which reliability was discussed and the proportion of expert evidence found unreliable rose. These increases do not appear to be due to a mere shift in terminology: the proportion of challenged evidence excluded rose following *Daubert*, indicating that the change in standards had real impacts. While the standards appear to be more stringent than what existed earlier, we do not know whether they have led to improvements in the quality of evidence admitted or to exclusion of evidence that should have been admitted. Our findings also suggest that the change in standards was not limited to a relatively small number of judges. However, additional information is needed to determine how evenly the changes were spread across the federal bench.

Judges Also Appear to Have Scrutinized Relevance, Qualifications, and Other Considerations That Enter into the Admission Decision More Closely

The *Daubert* decision did not change the standards for the relevance of expert evidence, the expert's qualifications, and other considerations that enter into a judge's assessment of whether to admit expert evidence, but it did affirm that judges should act as gatekeepers. Our findings suggest that judges scrutinized evidence with increasing care after *Daubert* with respect to these criteria. We found that the success rate for challenges based on all criteria (i.e., the percentage of evidence rated unfavorably when the criterion was addressed) rose after *Daubert*, although the increases did not always achieve statistical significance. It appears that once judges started acting as more-active gatekeepers, they more carefully examined relevance, qualifications, and other considerations for admitting evidence, in addition to reliability.

Challenges to Expert Evidence Became Increasingly Fatal to Cases

Challenges to expert evidence increasingly resulted in summary judgment after *Daubert*. We did not determine whether summary judgments disposed of some or all of the issues in each case, but nearly 90 percent of the summary judgments went against plaintiffs, making it likely that challenges to plaintiffs' evidence increasingly resulted in case dismissal. The increase in summary judgment requests may reflect broader trends in litigation practices that have little to do with *Daubert*. But *Daubert* may have led challengers to expand their challenges to the point where they increasingly challenged the entire basis of the case. *Daubert* also may have induced a shift from dismissals based on insufficient evidence to dismissals based on inadmissible evidence.

The Parties Responded to the Change in Standards

The parties proposing expert evidence and the parties challenging expert evidence appear to have responded gradually to the change in standards. After initially rising following *Daubert*, both the percentage of challenged evidence found unreliable and the percentage of challenged evidence excluded declined. This suggests that parties proposing expert evidence either did not propose or withdrew evidence that did not meet the new standards, or better tailored the evidence that they did propose to the new standards. Challengers, emboldened by higher success rates, also may have challenged more evidence. Casting a wider net would pull in challenges that are less likely to succeed, thus reducing the proportion of challenged evidence found unreliable.

Judges Increasingly Focused on Theory, Methods, and Procedures Underlying Expert Evidence

Our analysis suggests that judges were initially uncertain about the proper scope of their assessment and how to go about assessing reliability. In making reliability assessments, they at first focused on the five factors mentioned in the *Daubert* decision. Over time, however, as judges gained experience in evaluating reliability and as appellate court opinions clarified their authority, they appear to have felt less compelled to address each *Daubert* factor and to have paid increasing attention to more-general issues important to addressing reliability. Of particular note was the rapid rise in the frequency with which judges addressed the clarity and coherence of the expert's explanation of the theory, methods, and procedures underlying the evidence.

General Acceptance Was No Longer Sufficient by Itself for Admission of Evidence, But Lack of General Acceptance Remained an Important Barrier to Admission

Our findings suggest that general acceptance was not commonly used as a standard for deciding whether to admit expert evidence prior to *Daubert*, but that when it was used, it was a sufficient condition for admission. That is, evidence found to be generally accepted was nearly always admitted (assuming it did not fail on other criteria, such as relevance). This was not the situation after *Daubert*, however: judges sometimes found evidence unreliable even when they determined it to be generally accepted. This post-*Daubert* exclusion of evidence found to be generally accepted is another indication that judges were investigating the methods, theory, and procedures underlying the evidence itself.

Our findings also suggest that lack of general acceptance was as much a barrier to admission after *Daubert* as before, and perhaps an even greater barrier. Thus, there is no indication that it became easier for novel evidence not generally accepted in the relevant expert community to be admitted after *Daubert*.

Judges Increasingly Examined All Types of Expert Evidence, Not Just "Hard" Science

The *Daubert* decision was issued in the context of evidence based on toxicology studies, and the Supreme Court did not explicitly discuss whether the decision applied to all expert evidence. In the early years after *Daubert*, there was uncertainty over the breadth of its applicability. We found that while judges appear to have initially focused on the "hard," or physical, sciences, they soon began to examine the reliability of expert evidence in other substantive areas as well. Following *Daubert*, the proportion of challenged evidence found unreliable peaked first for evidence based on the physical sciences, but the proportions of challenged evidence found unreliable for evidence based on other substantive areas began to rise soon thereafter. It appears that once judges started evaluating reliability, they gradually began looking at all types of expert evidence. In its 1999 *Kumho* decision, the Supreme Court affirmed that the *Daubert* decision applied to all types of expert evidence. *Kumho* appears to have endorsed practices that were already in place in many federal courts.

Expert Evidence Based on Engineering and Technology and on Health Care and Medicine Has Increasingly Become the Target of Challenges

The composition of challenged evidence has changed since *Daubert*. In the first several years after the decision, the proportion of challenged evidence that was based on the physical sciences rose. In subsequent years, however, this proportion fell and was replaced by higher proportions of evidence from engineering and technology and from health care and medicine. This initial rise in challenges to evidence from the physical sciences and later rises in challenges to evidence from the other two areas parallel the changes over time in the percentage of these types of evidence found unreliable after *Daubert*. This suggests that parties challenging evidence initially focused on the physical sciences after *Daubert* and then moved to other areas. Challengers may have moved to other areas because proposers improved the quality of the evidence based on physical science in response to the increased scrutiny. Challengers also may have moved to other areas because *Daubert*'s applicability to all expert evidence, not just evidence from the physical sciences, became better established over time.

8.2   NEXT STEPS

Our analysis of federal district court opinions provides strong evidence that the *Daubert* decision changed how federal district court judges assess expert evidence in civil cases. It appears that judges are indeed doing what they were directed to do by the Supreme Court: increasingly acting as gatekeepers for reliability and relevance, examining the methods and reasoning underlying the evidence, and viewing general acceptance as only one of many factors to be considered in their reliability assessments. The rise that occurred in both the proportion of evidence found unreliable and the proportion of challenged evidence excluded suggests that the standards for admitting evidence have tightened. The subsequent fall in these proportions suggests that parties proposing evidence, and perhaps parties challenging evidence, have responded to the change in standards.

However, even though there is convincing evidence that practices and standards have changed, our findings do not allow us to determine whether the changes have resulted in better outcomes. Several questions warrant further exploration:

How Well Are Judges Performing the Gatekeeper Function?

While judges may be more actively evaluating reliability, we do not know if they are doing it in ways that produce better outcomes. Judges may feel compelled to evaluate reliability and yet not be knowledgeable enough in the relevant field to make accurate determinations.[1] Evidence could thus be excluded because it is difficult to understand rather than because it is unreliable. And evidence could be admitted because the judge does not understand a flaw in an argument rather than because it is reliable.

It is difficult to measure the performance of court policies for evaluating and admitting evidence. Reliability is not an easy characteristic to measure, but given the importance of expert

---

[1]The findings of Gatowski et al. (2001) that were discussed in Section 1 provide cause for concern. Their study concluded that state court judges did not have a good understanding of the scientific meaning of the *Daubert* standards or how to apply them.

evidence to case outcomes and the stakes involved, its evaluation is a task worth the effort. One promising approach is to assemble panels of experts to evaluate expert evidence in a sample of cases. The experts would evaluate the reliability of both admitted evidence and excluded evidence so as to understand how well the screening process is working. The results of such an evaluation could be the basis of a report card on how well judges are performing the gatekeeper function.

How Has *Daubert* Affected Case Outcomes?

We have limited information on what effect *Daubert* has had on case outcomes. We found that the proportion of challenges resulting in summary judgment rose after *Daubert*, but we cannot be certain what role *Daubert* played in the increase or whether cases dismissed because evidence was excluded would have been dismissed on other grounds had there not been a change in the standards for reliability. To better understand how *Daubert* has changed the standards for admitting expert evidence and the consequences of the changes, we need a more complete understanding of how exclusions of expert evidence affect case outcomes. For example, we might examine how likely it is for cases to settle or be dropped once evidence is excluded, or whether plaintiffs' attorneys are able to retool an expert and succeed in admitting similar evidence in subsequent cases.

Assembling the histories of a representative sample of cases involving expert evidence would provide a rich set of data on these and related questions. The lawyers on both sides of a case could be surveyed to characterize what evidence was introduced, what was challenged, and what was admitted and excluded. The subsequent response of the parties to exclusion or admission could then be recorded.

What Are the Time and Dollar Costs of the Current System for Screening Expert Evidence?

This study touched only briefly on the time needed to bring and resolve challenges to expert evidence and was silent on the dollar costs both to litigants and the courts. Time and dollar costs are, of course, central concerns of a judicial system that aims to be speedy and efficient, and they are also important to justice. A system that takes a very long time to resolve disputes may discourage valid claims and prevent parties from receiving the compensation they are due. And a system in which it is very expensive to prepare expert evidence and to survive *Daubert* challenges may discourage injured parties from bringing small but valid claims.

Data on the time needed to bring and resolve challenges and the dollar costs incurred are best collected from the lawyers involved in the cases. This information could be gathered as part of the lawyer survey described above. Judicial time records could also be examined to quantify the judicial resources involved.

Answers to questions such as these are central to understanding how well the current system for screening expert evidence is working. They will help policymakers better understand what further improvements might be warranted. They will also help policymakers understand the consequences of past changes so that if and when they want to make new changes, they can apply past experience in a positive manner.

A. CHARACTERISTICS OF SAMPLE OF OPINIONS, ELEMENTS OF EVIDENCE, EXPERTS, AND LITIGANTS

In this appendix, we provide tabulations of the raw data extracted from the 399 federal district court opinions on challenges to expert evidence. Much of the analysis in the body of the report holds constant the case type, substantive area of evidence, and appellate circuit in which the federal court lies. Here, we do not control for variation in these factors over time. For simplicity, we report statistics for the opinions issued pre-*Daubert* (1/80–6/93), post-*Daubert* (7/93–6/99), and for the entire period (1/80–6/99). These data are presented in the following order:

- characteristics of underlying disputes
- characteristics of challenged evidence
- characteristics of litigants
- characteristics of experts
- characteristics of challenges to expert evidence.

CHARACTERISTICS OF UNDERLYING DISPUTES

We here describe the disputes underlying the challenged evidence. These are thus opinion-level data, and the tabulations are based on 399 observations. Each opinion can address multiple elements of evidence, and the opinion-level data are common to all the elements of evidence addressed in the particular opinion.

Geographic Variation

Figure A.1 compares the distribution of the 399 opinions by federal appellate circuit with the distribution of all federal civil cases (excluding prisoners' petitions, social security, and debt cases) that were open at some point between 1980 and 1997.[1] Opinions from the Third and Seventh Circuits are substantially overrepresented in our sample of 399 opinions.[2] This is primarily due to a relatively large number of opinions from the Eastern District of Pennsylvania in the Third Circuit and the Northern District of Illinois in the Seventh Circuit. Both of the districts were among the first for which unreported opinions were also posted in Westlaw.

---

[1]The data on all federal civil cases are based on analysis of the Federal Filing Database, produced by the Administrative Office of the U.S. Courts, Statistical Analysis and Report Division.

[2]Note that the distribution of cases with expert evidence by circuit may differ from the distribution of all civil cases by circuit.

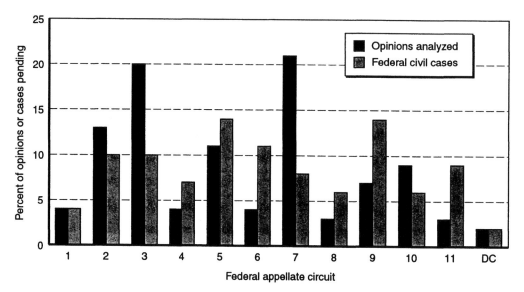

Figure A.1—Comparison of 399 Opinions Analyzed and All Federal Civil Cases Open at Some Point Between 1980 and 1997, by Federal Appellate Circuit

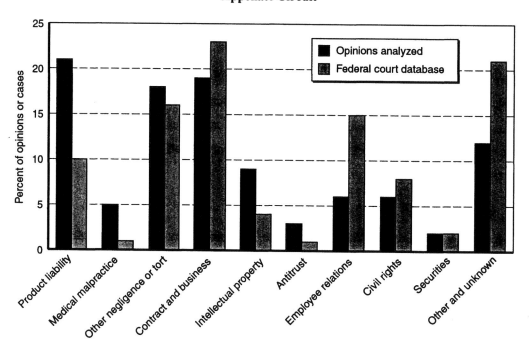

Figure A.2—Distribution of Opinions Analyzed and Civil Cases Pending After 1980, by Case Type

Case Type

Figure A.2 compares the distribution of case type for the 399 opinions we analyzed with that for all federal cases that were open at some point between 1980 and 1997. The figure suggests that challenges to expert evidence occur more frequently in product liability, medical malpractice, and intellectual property cases than in other types of cases.

Table A.1 reports the change in case mix over time. Note that the case types shown in Figure A.2 have been grouped into larger categories in the table because of the smaller number of observations in each time period. For comparison, Table A.2 reports trends in the case mix for all federal civil cases pending at some point during each period.

Table A.1

Case Mix of Challenged Evidence
(percent)

	Opinion Date[a]			
Case Type	1/80–6/89 (N=68)	7/89–6/93 (N=87)	7/93–6/96 (N=106)	7/96–6/99 (N=124)
Bodily injury and property damage torts				
Product liability	22	20	17	26
Other BI and PD	19	34	23	20
Contract cases and business torts	15	17	25	19
Intellectual property	13	8	7	9
Employee relations/ discrimination	6	2	6	9
Civil rights (not employment related)	6	6	6	8
Other	19	13	17	10
Total	100	100	100	100

[a]Case type not discussed in 14 of the 399 opinions.

Table A.2

Case Mix for All Federal Cases Pending During Each Time Period
(percent)

Case Type	1/80–6/89 (N=1,590K)	7/89–6/93 (N=799K)	7/93–6/96 (N=668K)	7/96–9/97 (N=416K)
Bodily injury and property damage torts				
Product Liability	8	12	14	18
Other BI and PD	18	16	15	16
Contracts and business torts	27	22	17	16
Intellectual property	3	3	4	4
Employee relations/ discrimination	13	15	19	20
Civil rights (not employment related)	7	8	10	10
Other	23	24	20	16
Total	100	100	100	100

SOURCE: Federal Filing Database, Administrative Office of the U.S. Courts, Statistical Analysis and Report Division.

Table A.3

Characteristics of Cases in Which Evidence Challenged
(percent of 399 opinions)

	1/80–6/93 (N=163)	7/93–6/99 (N=236)	Entire Sample Period (N=399)
A. Nature of Alleged Injury			
Physical or emotional human harm	55	50	52
Financial injury	38	42	41
Damage to real or personal property	7	8	8
Not discussed	4	3	4
Total[a]	104	103	105
B. Stage of Case at Time of Opinion			
Pre-trial	63	76	71
Trial or post-trial	32	16	23
Not discussed	5	8	6
Total	100	100	100
C. Expected Trier of Fact			
Jury	53	49	50
Judge	11	7	9
Not discussed	36	44	41
Total	100	100	100
D. Use of Neutral Experts by Judge to Help Evaluate Experts			
Judge used a neutral expert	2	0	1
No indication from opinion that judge used a neutral expert	98	100	99
Total	100	100	100
E. Involvement of Magistrate Judge in Hearing the Evidence			
Magistrate judge involved	8	8	8
No indication from opinion that magistrate judge involved	92	92	92
Total	100	100	100

[a]Alleged injuries may fall into more than one category, so percentages may add up to more than 100 percent.

Other Case Characteristics

Table A.3 provides an overview of other key characteristics of the 399 cases underlying the opinions. Of the 399 opinions, 163 were issued before *Daubert* and 236 after *Daubert*.

CHARACTERISTICS OF CHALLENGED EVIDENCE

Table A.4 presents characteristics of the 601 elements of evidence. It describes the party proposing the evidence, the party challenging the evidence, and the purpose of the testimony or evidence. (The substantive area of evidence—physical science, engineering and technology, etc.—is discussed in Subsection 3.2.)

Table A.4

Characteristics of Challenged Evidence
(percent of 601 elements of evidence)

		1/80-6/93 (N=226)	7/93-6/99 (N=375)	Entire Sample Period (N=601)
A.	**Party Proposing Evidence**			
	Plaintiff	79	81	80
	Defendant	19	18	19
	Not discussed	2	1	1
	Total	100	100	100
B.	**Party Challenging Evidence**			
	Plaintiff	17	17	17
	Defendant	73	77	76
	Court	6	2	4
	Not discussed	4	4	4
	Total	100	100	100
C.	**Purpose of Testimony or Evidence**			
	Cause of injury or condition	31	35	33
	Existence or extent of physical or physiological injury	7	6	6
	Existence or extent of psychological or emotional injury	1	2	2
	Existence or extent of damage to real or personal property	3	5	4
	Existence or extent of financial injury	18	17	18
	Characterization of professional standards	6	3	4
	Characterization of industry or regulatory standards	15	7	10
	Design, manufacture, or testing of a product, structure or device	6	9	8
	Knowledge, intent, or state of mind of a party	5	9	7
	Other and not discussed	8	7	8
	Total	100	100	100

CHARACTERISTICS OF LITIGANTS

Table A.5 reports the affiliations of the litigants. Up to four plaintiffs and up to four defendants (the first four) were coded for each of the 399 opinions analyzed. The result is that we coded 602 plaintiff-opinion pairs and 718 defendant-opinion pairs. The numbers of unique plaintiffs and defendants in our data may be lower than these numbers because the same litigant might be named in more than one opinion.

CHARACTERISTICS OF EXPERTS

We recorded information on the experts named in each of the 399 opinions (see Table A.6). In some opinions, no experts were named; in others, multiple experts were named. Overall we collected information on 569 expert-opinion pairs, which is likely more than the number of

Table A.5

Affiliations of Litigants
(percent of plaintiff-opinion or defendant-opinion pairs)

		1/80–6/93	7/93–6/99	Entire Sample Period
A.	**Affiliation of Plaintiff**	(N=244)	(N=358)	(N=602)
	Government[a]	6	2	3
	Business	21	21	21
	Non-profit	1	1	1
	Individual	71	75	73
	Not discussed	<1	<1	<1
	Total	100	100	100
B.	**Affiliation of Defendant**	(N=276)	(N=442)	(N=718)
	Government[a]	13	13	13
	Business	68	71	70
	Non-profit	2	1	1
	Individual	14	14	14
	Not discussed	2	<1	1
	Total	100	100	100

[a]Includes government agencies and government employees.

Table A.6

Characteristics of Experts
(percent of expert-opinion pairs identified in 399 opinions)

	1/80–6/93 (N=206)	7/93–6/99 (N=363)	Entire Sample Period (N=569)
A. Degree Attained (as described in opinion)[a]			
Doctorate	23	27	25
MD	16	16	16
JD or LLB	9	3	5
Masters	3	4	4
Other	5	9	8
Not discussed	50	46	47
B. Gender			
Female	6	6	6
Male	87	89	88
Could not be ascertained from name or pronouns	7	5	6
Total	100	100	100

[a]An expert may have more than one degree, so percentages in this panel sum to more than 100.

unique experts because some experts may appear in multiple opinions. The experts named in an opinion might be involved in some or all of the elements of evidence addressed in that opinion.

CHARACTERISTICS OF CHALLENGES TO EXPERT EVIDENCE

Table A.7 lists the frequencies with which different criteria were addressed, the success rates for the challenges on each criterion, and the frequencies with which the evidence was rated negatively on the various criteria. Panel A reports the percentage of the elements of evidence (226 pre-*Daubert*, 375 post-*Daubert*) for which the various criteria were addressed. In panel B, the sample size in each cell is the number of elements of evidence for which the criterion was addressed pre-*Daubert*, post-*Daubert*, or for the whole sample. Similar to panel A, panel C reports the percentage of the elements of evidence rated unfavorably on each criteria.

Table A.8 reports the frequencies with which the various reliability factors were addressed and rated unfavorably pre- and post-*Daubert*.

Table A.7
Criteria Addressed and Evidence Rated Unfavorably
(percent of elements of evidence)

		1/80–6/93	7/93–6/99	Entire Sample Period
A.	**Criterion Addressed**	(N=226)	(N=375)	(N=601)
	Reliability	40	53	48
	Relevance	47	38	42
	Qualifications	30	32	31
	Other considerations	25	17	20
B.	**Evidence Rated Unfavorably on Criterion Given Criterion Addressed (Success Rate)**			
	Reliability	49	54	53
		(N=91)	(N=199)	(N=290)
	Relevance	51	56	54
		(N=107)	(N=144)	(N=251)
	Qualifications	21	29	30
		(N=68)	(N=120)	(N=188)
	Other	29	43	36
		(N=56)	(N=63)	(N=119)
C.	**Evidence Rated Unfavorably on Criterion**	(N=226)	(N=375)	(N=601)
	Reliability	20	29	26
	Relevance	25	22	23
	Qualifications	9	9	9
	Other considerations	7	7	7

Table A.8

Data on Frequency with Which Reliability Factors Addressed and Proportion of Evidence Rated Unfavorably
(percent of elements of evidence)

Reliability Factor	Factor Addressed			Evidence Rated Unfavorably on Factor		
	1/80–6/93 (N=226)	7/93–6/99 (N=375)	1/80–6/99 (N=601)	1/80–6/93 (N=226)	7/93–6/99 (N=375)	1/80–6/99 (N=601)
1. Peer review and publication	4	9	7	2	6	4
2. General acceptance in relevant expert community	5	13	10	4	7	6
3. Potential for testing or actual testing	1	9	6	1	7	5
4. Known or potential rate of error	2	6	4	1	4	3
5. Existence and maintenance of standards controlling use of technique or method	2	7	5	1	4	3
6. Clarity and coherence of expert's explanation of theory, methods, procedures	8	16	13	5	13	10
7. Proper extrapolation	8	10	9	5	9	7
8. Breadth of facts, data, or studies underlying analysis	18	15	16	10	9	9
9. Reliance on verifiable evidence or data	9	11	10	6	9	8
10. Control for or consideration of confounding factors	5	8	7	4	7	6
11. Use of facts or data reasonably relied on by experts in field	11	5	8	5	1	3
12. Consistency of theory or findings with other studies, principles, or experts in field	4	5	5	3	3	3
13. Statistical significance of findings	2	2	2	2	1	1
14. Existence of real-world data to support theory	6	4	5	4	3	3
15. Court-appointed neutral expert's evaluation of evidence	0	<1	<1	0	0	0
16. Purpose for which research was conducted	2	2	2	2	1	1
17. Reputation of expert	2	2	2	1	1	1

Table A.9 provides descriptive statistics on summary judgments. It reports the frequencies with which summary judgments were requested and granted, and it characterizes the evidence associated with the summary judgment requests.

Table A.9

Data on Summary Judgments
(percent of elements of evidence)

	1/80–6/93	7/93–6/99	Entire Sample Period
A. All Elements of Evidence	(N=226)	(N=375)	(N=601)
Summary judgment requested	24	42	32
Summary judgment granted	10	20	15
B. Elements of Evidence Involved in a Request for Summary Judgment	(N=79)	(N=114)	(N=193)
Party proposing evidence			
Plaintiff	89	88	88
Defendant	9	11	10
Unknown	3	1	2
Purpose of testimony			
Cause of injury or condition	44	54	50
Existence or extent of injury	18	9	12
Other or unknown	38	37	38
C. Elements of Evidence Involved in a Grant of Summary Judgment	(N=35)	(N=54)	(N=89)
Party proposing evidence			
Plaintiff	91	96	94
Defendant	6	4	4
Unknown	3	0	1
Purpose of testimony			
Cause of injury or condition	46	69	60
Existence or extent of injury	20	9	11
Other or unknown	34	22	29

B. STATISTICAL APPROACH FOR ANALYZING CHANGES OVER TIME IN OUTCOMES OF INTEREST

This appendix describes the statistical approach we used to estimate changes over time in the outcomes of interest. To illustrate the approach, we report results for the proportion of challenged evidence in which reliability was addressed, the proportion of challenged evidence found unreliable given that reliability was addressed (the success rate for reliability challenges), and the proportion of challenged evidence found unreliable. Similar estimates were made for the other outcomes of interest.

We modeled the outcomes of interest using a logistic model. The model includes case type, substantive area of challenged evidence, appellate circuit in which district court lies, and time period in which opinion was issued. Each characteristic (case type, substantive area of evidence, appellate circuit, time period) is broken down into several categories, and one category is chosen as the reference category for each characteristic.

In the logistic model, the outcome is a Bernoulli random variable taking on the values of 0 or 1. The expected value of the outcome, $E(Y_i) = \pi_i$, is the probability that the outcome for the ith observation takes the value 1 and is a function of several explanatory variables:

$$\pi_i = \frac{\exp(B'X_i)}{1+\exp(B'X_i)} \tag{1}$$

where

$$B'X_i = \beta_0 + \sum_{j=1}^{D-1}\beta_j d_{ji} + \sum_{k=1}^{C-1}\alpha_k c_{ki} + \sum_{m=1}^{A-1}\delta_m a_{mi} + \sum_{n=1}^{T-1}\lambda_n t_{ni} \tag{2}$$

and

$$d_{ji} = \begin{cases} 1 & \text{if the district court for observation } i \text{ lies in appellate circuit } j \\ 0 & \text{otherwise} \end{cases}$$

$$c_{ki} = \begin{cases} 1 & \text{if the case type for observation } i \text{ falls in category } k \\ 0 & \text{otherwise} \end{cases}$$

$$a_{mi} = \begin{cases} 1 & \text{if the substantive area of evidence for observation } i \text{ falls in category } m \\ 0 & \text{otherwise} \end{cases}$$

$$t_{ni} = \begin{cases} 1 & \text{if the opinion date for observation } i \text{ falls in period } n \\ 0 & \text{otherwise} \end{cases}$$

D, C, A, and T are the number of appellate circuit, case type, substantive area of evidence, and time categories, respectively. A detailed discussion of this type of logit model can be found in Agresti (1990).

Some of the elements of evidence come from the same opinion and the errors for these observations may be correlated. We accounted for this by estimating the coefficients using a Generalized Estimating Equation (GEE) with a working independence correlation matrix and the empirical standard errors (Zeger and Liang, 1986). The SAS GENMOD procedure was used to estimate the equations.

Table B.1 reports the results for reliability. The second and third columns show the results for the proportion of evidence in which reliability is addressed. The outcome of interest is the probability that reliability is discussed for an element of evidence. Case type is broken down into nine categories, with "other and unknown" serving as the reference category. Substantive area of evidence is broken down into six categories, again with "other and unknown" as the reference category. Time is broken down into seven periods; 7/91–6/93 serves as the reference period. The federal district courts are divided into 11 appellate circuits. The Third Circuit serves as the reference category, and the DC Circuit is combined with the Fourth Circuit because of the small number of observations in the DC Circuit. The model is estimated on 601 elements of evidence. The last two columns of Table B.1 report the results for the proportion of challenged evidence found unreliable. Table B.2 reports results for the proportion of evidence found unreliable given that reliability was addressed.

We used the estimated models to predict changes in the outcomes of interest over time while holding case type, substantive area of evidence, and appellate circuit constant. To do this, we set the indicator variables in Eq. (2) for product liability cases and evidence from the physical sciences equal to one and set the other indicator variables to zero.

We also identified changes in the frequency with which reliability was addressed and evidence was found reliable by geographic region. To do this, we divided the United States into four regions. Table B.3 reports the appellate circuits and number of elements of evidence in each of the four regions. It also reports the predicted probabilities when case type and substantive area of evidence are held constant.[3]

Table B.1

Logit Model for Reliability of Elements of Evidence

Variable[a]	Reliability Addressed		Evidence Found Unreliable	
	Coeff.	Std. Err.	Coeff.	Std. Err.
Intercept	-1.2454**	0.5609	-3.3342**	0.8252
Case type				
Product liability	0.6701*	0.3587	1.1614**	0.45
Toxic tort	0.9727**	0.4660	1.705**	0.5479
Professional negligence	-0.0791	0.3879	0.0516	0.534
Other negligence	0.0867	0.4513	-0.017	0.5994
Business transactions	-0.2262	0.3502	0.2579	0.4399
Intellectual property	-0.2300	0.4313	0.5976	0.5149
Employee relations	-0.6328	0.5382	1.1614	0.45
Civil rights	-0.1221	0.4789	1.705**	0.5479
Area of evidence				
Health care and medicine	0.5057	0.4445	0.5082	0.5756
Engineering and technology	0.0300	0.4500	0.7761	0.4773
Physical science	1.3457**	0.5241	1.1612**	0.6288
Social and behavioral science	1.1444**	0.4433	0.6572**	0.6298
Business, law, and pub. admin.	-0.2007	0.4346	1.7148	0.7128
Time variables				
1/80-6/89	0.6687*	0.3890	0.8125	0.5027
7/89-6/91	0.1154	0.4068	-0.0963	0.5772
7/93-6/95	0.3841	0.3789	0.5075	0.5088
7/95-6/96	0.6791*	0.4007	0.8056	0.5135
7/96-6/97	1.3015**	0.4259	1.2976**	0.502
7/97-6/98	1.1698**	0.4073	1.0418**	0.5166
7/98-6/99	0.7808*	0.4093	0.7488	0.5194
Number of observations	601		601	

NOTE: Single asterisk (*) means difference is statistically significant at 10 percent; double asterisk (**) means difference is statistically significant at 5 percent.

[a]Coefficients for circuit court dummy variables not reported in order to save space.

---

[3]We also checked to see whether there were differences between the 11 districts that Westlaw singled out as reporting a higher proportion of written opinions (see Subsection 3.1) and other districts. We found similar patterns in the two sets of districts.

Table B.2

**Logit Model for Evidence Found Unreliable
When Reliability Addressed**

Variable[a]	Coeff.	Std. Err.
Intercept	-2.004**	0.8521
Case type		
Product liability	1.2264**	0.5282
Toxic tort	1.7089**	0.6334
Professional negligence	0.2685	0.6407
Other negligence	-0.251	0.7273
Business transactions	0.5528	0.5407
Intellectual property	1.2804**	0.6489
Employee relations	1.4341*	0.8525
Civil rights	1.1921**	0.5492
Area of evidence		
Health care and medicine	1.2368**	0.6231
Engineering and technology	0.6114	0.6182
Physical science	1.1374*	0.6046
Social and behavioral science	1.0395	0.6532
Business, law, and pub. admin.	1.4756**	0.7144
Time variables		
1/80-6/89	0.4045	0.5768
7/89-6/91	-0.4625	0.7203
7/93-6/95	0.4474	0.5766
7/95-6/96	0.5797	0.5906
7/96-6/97	0.6309	0.5509
7/97-6/98	0.3835	0.5841
7/98-6/99	0.1079	0.6741
Number of observations	290	

NOTE: Single asterisk (*) means difference is statistically significant at 10 percent; double asterisk (**) means difference is statistically significant at 5 percent.
[a]Coefficients for circuit court dummy variables not reported in order to save space.

Table B.3

**Proportion of Challenged Evidence in Which Reliability Addressed and
Proportion Found Unreliable, by Geographic Area
(predicted percent with case type and area of evidence held constant)**

			Opinion Date				
Geographic Region		N	1/80–6/89	7/89–6/93	7/93–6/95	7/95–6/97	7/97–6/99
A.	**Reliability Addressed**						
	Northeast (circuits 1,2,3)	227	80	68	87**	86**	82
	Central (circuits 6,7)	149	88	90	83	98**	98**
	South (circuits 4,5,11,DC)	121	98**	84	94	83	93
	West (circuits 8,9,10)	104	76	66	55	89**	87**
B.	**Evidence Found Unreliable**						
	Northeast (circuits 1,2,3)	227	43	38	53	61	52
	Midwest (circuits 6,7)	149	46	23	35	64**	72**
	South (circuits 4,5,11,DC)	121	91**	57	64	51	49
	West (circuits 8,9,10)	104	52	36	71	80**	68

NOTES: (1) Case types reduced to four categories and toxic tort and product liability cases combined in statistical analyses. (2) Reference period used to calculate statistical significance of changes is shaded. (3) Single asterisk (*) indicates difference from reference period is statistically significant at 10 percent; double asterisk (**) indicates difference from reference period is statistically significant at 5 percent.

C. EVIDENCE THAT *DAUBERT* WAS APPLIED TO CASES FILED BEFORE JULY 1993

Table C.1 provides data illustrating that the *Daubert* decision applied to cases filed both before and after it was issued (June 1993). The third column examines those elements of evidence for which reliability was addressed. For various opinion dates, it shows the percentage of the time that the cases underlying the elements of evidence were filed pre-*Daubert*. The last column shows the same percentage for elements of evidence for which reliability was not addressed. If *Daubert* had been applied mainly to cases filed after June 1993, the percentages in the third column (for opinions dated post-June 1993) would most likely be much lower than those in the final column.[4] While the percentages of cases filed pre-*Daubert* in which reliability was addressed are somewhat lower for opinions issued from July 1993 to June 1995 and July 1997 to June 1999, the same percentage is much higher for opinions issued from July 1995 to June 1997. This implies that cases filed pre-*Daubert* were also subject to increased scrutiny after the decision was issued.

Table C.1

Percentage of Elements of Evidence from Cases Filed Pre-*Daubert*, by Opinion Date

Opinion Date	Elements of Evidence for Which Reliability Addressed		Elements of Evidence for Which Reliability Not Addressed	
	N	Percent Filed Pre-*Daubert*	N	Percent Filed Pre-*Daubert*
1/80–6/89	42	100	49	100
7/89–6/93	48	100	85	100
7/93–6/95	58	69	82	77
7/95–6/97	69	64	39	38
7/97–6/99	72	11	54	24
Total	289	63	309	73

[4]We did not examine how the percentage of opinions in which reliability was addressed varied by filing date because the length of time that a case has been open varies with filing date.

D. STATISTICAL ANALYSIS OF CHANGES IN THE DECISIVENESS OF GENERAL ACCEPTANCE

We used a logistic model to examine whether the decisiveness of general acceptance has changed over time. The outcome variables are whether the element of evidence was found unreliable and whether the challenged evidence was excluded. The key explanatory variables are (1) whether the evidence was rated unfavorably on general acceptance and (2) whether the evidence was rated unfavorably on any other reliability factor. The two variables were interacted with time to test whether the decisiveness of general acceptance and that of the other reliability factors have changed. A positive coefficient on the interaction between time and a reliability factor means that the probability that the element of evidence will be found unreliable when it is rated negatively on that factor (holding its rating on the other factors constant) increased during the time period. As before, dummy variables for case type, substantive area of evidence, and appellate circuit were included to control for a variety of evidence-specific characteristics that remain constant over time. The model was also estimated allowing for correlation among the errors for elements of evidence coming from the same opinion.

The logit model has the same form as the model described in Appendix B, but here the explanatory variables are

$$B'X_i = \beta_0 + \sum_{j=1}^{D-1} \beta_j d_{ji} + \sum_{k=1}^{C-1} \alpha_k c_{ki} + \sum_{m=1}^{A-1} \delta_m a_{mi} + \sum_{n=1}^{2} \lambda_n f_{ni} + \sum_{n=1}^{2} \xi_n t_i * f_{ni} \qquad (2)$$

where

$$f_{ni} = \begin{cases} 1 & \text{if evidence for observation } i \text{ is rated negatively on any reliablity factor in group } n \\ 0 & \text{otherwise} \end{cases}$$

$$t_i = \begin{cases} 1 & \text{if the opinion for observation } i \text{ was issued prior to } Daubert \\ 0 & \text{otherwise} \end{cases}$$

and the other variables are as defined in Appendix B.

Table D.1 reports the results. The second and third columns show the results for whether the evidence elements are found unreliable. As can be seen, after *Daubert*, general acceptance is a good predictor of whether evidence was found reliable when ratings on other reliability factors are held constant. (The coefficient 3.5699 has the expected sign and is statistically significant at 10 percent.) Prior to *Daubert*, the coefficient on general acceptance (the sum of 3.5699 and

Table D.1

Logit Model for Change in Decisiveness of General Acceptance

Variable[a]	Found Unreliable		Evidence Excluded	
	Coeff.	Std. Err.	Coeff.	Std. Err.
Intercept	-7.6937	1.0726**	-1.406**	0.6069
Case type				
Product liability	-0.8151	0.8692	0.4377	0.4058
Toxic tort	-0.3761	1.4006	1.526**	0.7349
Professional negligence	-0.9202	0.9014	-0.0675	0.4392
Other negligence	-3.1167	1.1495**	0.4542	0.5208
Business transactions	0.6839	0.8893	0.6402*	0.3757
Intellectual property	-0.8626	0.8086	0.308	0.444
Employee relations	1.0275	1.3606	0.5573	0.5091
Civil rights	1.7217	1.434	0.958*	0.5289
Area of evidence				
Health care and medicine	3.1453	0.7735**	-0.0507	0.5687
Engineering and technology	2.8323	0.8988**	0.3883	0.5413
Physical science	2.9819	1.0537**	-0.6279	0.6787
Social and behavioral science	2.095	1.1021*	0.2856	0.5624
Business, law, and pub. admin.	1.9121	1.0005*	0.7844	0.5195
General acceptance	3.5699	1.8831*	1.9123*	1.1562
Other factors	7.2385	0.7951**	2.7861**	0.5059
(General acceptance) x (pre-*Daubert*)	-4.6058	2.7479*	-2.7399	1.891
(Other factors) x (pre-*Daubert*)	0.7941	0.6747	0.687	0.7928
Number of observations	601		601	

NOTE: Single asterisk (*) means difference is statistically significant at 10 percent; double asterisk (**) means difference is statistically significant at 5 percent.

[a]Coefficients for circuit court dummy variables not reported in order to save space.

—4.6058) is small, not the expected sign, and not statistically significant. This implies that prior to *Daubert*, general acceptance is not a good predictor of whether evidence was found unreliable when whether it was rated unfavorably on the other reliability factors is held constant.[5] There is no statistically significant difference in the coefficients on the other reliability factors pre- versus post-*Daubert*.

Table D.2 repeats Table 5.3 for the percentage of evidence excluded (as opposed to found unreliable) according to how the evidence was rated on general acceptance. The patterns are similar to those for the percentage of evidence found unreliable. As shown in the last two

---

[5]We also tested for changes in the decisiveness of general acceptance before and after June 1995. We did this to increase the number of observations before the cutoff and because our findings suggest that changes in standards for admitting expert evidence were only gradually phased in during the first two years after *Daubert* (see, for example, Figure 7.1). The results using this later cutoff were very similar to those arrived at by splitting the sample at the *Daubert* decision.

columns of Table D.1, the logit results for decisiveness are similar whether the evidence was excluded or found unreliable. As before, no evidence that was found generally accepted was excluded pre-*Daubert*. Post-*Daubert*, however, 30 percent of evidence found generally accepted was excluded.

Table D.2

**Decisiveness of General Acceptance: Percentage of Evidence Excluded
for Different General Acceptance Ratings**

| | 1/80–6/95 | | 7/95–6/99 | |
Rating on General Acceptance	N	Percent Excluded	N	Percent Excluded
Favorable	4	0	20	30
Neutral	0	—	3	0
Unfavorable	8	88	27	96
Not addressed	214	51	325	52
Total	226	51	375	54